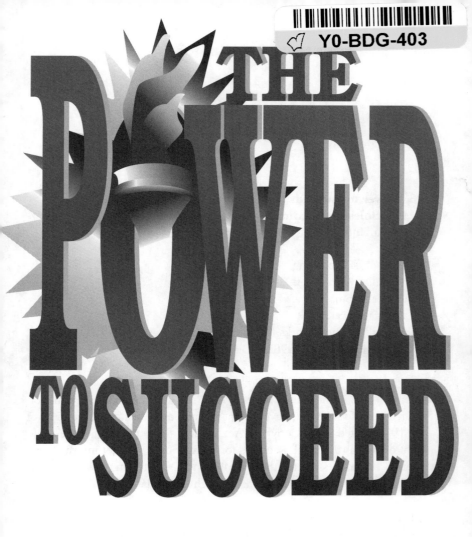

THE POWER TO SUCCEED

30 Principles for Maximizing Your Personal Effectiveness

Dr. Joe Rubino

The Power to Succeed:
30 Principles for Maximizing Your Personal Effectiveness
Dr. Joe Rubino

Vision Works Publishing,
First Edition ©Copyright 2002
By Dr. Joe Rubino
All rights reserved.
Published by Vision Works Publishing
888-821-3135 Fax: 630-982-2134
VisionWorksBooks@Email.com

ISBN 0-9678529-8-6   PB
Library of Congress Catalog Card Number: 00-191046

10 9 8 7 6 5 4 3

With this book YOU will:

- Uncover the secrets to accessing your personal power.
- Create a structure for maximizing your effectiveness with others.
- Learn to take total responsibility for everything in your life.
- Discover the key elements to accomplishment and how to reach your goals in record time.
- Reveal your life rules and discover how honoring your core values can help you maximize productivity.
- Complete your past and design your ideal future.
- Discover the keys to communicating effectively and intentionally.
- Stop complaining and start doing.
- Seize your personal power and conquer resignation in your life.
- Learn how to generate conversations that uncover new possibilities.
- See how embracing problems can lead to positive breakthroughs in life.
- Leave others whole while realizing the power of telling the truth.
- Learn how to develop the charisma necessary to attract others to you.

We attract people and situations into our lives, creating opportunities to take on what's next for our development. We can either choose to make the most of these opportunities and expand the person we are or we can ignore them and continue to maintain the status quo. We get to choose which it will be.

Dr. Joe Rubino

A Ph.D. program for living. I highly recommend it.

—Mike Smith
Founder, BridgeQuest, Inc.

I have a confession: I started reading **The Power to Succeed** *with the jaundiced eye of* "Been There. Done That." *(Borrowing the title of Joe's first book; Hey, Rubino and I share the same teachers. What's he gonna' tell me I don't already know...?) Well, shame on me — and kudos to the good doctor!* **The Power to Succeed** *shows you how to reveal and tap into your own power. It's an interactive book that has you change your mind and take positive action. This book reminded me of lots I'd forgotten and taught me lots new, too. Way to go, Joe— and... Thanks!*

—John Milton Fogg
Author, *The Greatest Networker in the World*
Founder Upline® and *Network Marketing Lifestyles* magazines

The Power to Succeed *books are life changing! This is one of the most effective self-study programs available to become more effective with others and more powerful in your life and your business. Fire up your personal power to succeed.*

—Jan Ruhe
Author, *True Leadership*

These books are the next best thing to taking a year-long transformational personal development course.

—Richard Brooke
Author, *Mach II With Your Hair on Fire*

This book is Dr. Joe's masterpiece! A brilliant system for reaching great heights. A road map to the principles of life that spell super-success for anyone who is willing to apply them. This book should be read — no, it should be devoured! — by everyone.

—Bob Burg
Author, *Winning Without Intimidation*

On rare occasion does something come along that would be considered life-altering. **The Power to Succeed** *books are just that. This is the most impactful and powerful self-study program available to become more effective and empowering with others and more centered and "ignited" in your life and your business. These books are the only substitute I have found powerful enough if you cannot take a year-long personal development course. They are on fire!*

—Doug Firebaugh
CEO, PassionFire International

DEDICATION

For Freda and Joe

The Rules For Being Human
Author Unknown

1. You will receive a body. You may like it or hate it, but it will be yours for the entire period this time around.

2. You will learn lessons. You are enrolled in a full-time informal school called life. Each day in this school you will have the opportunity to learn lessons. You may like the lessons or think them irrelevant and stupid.

3. There are no mistakes, only lessons. Growth is a process of trial and error: experimentation. The failed experiments are as much a part of the process as the experiments that ultimately "work."

4. A lesson is repeated until learned. A lesson will be presented to you in various forms until you have learned it. When you have learned it, then you can go on to the next lesson.

5. Learning lessons does not end. There is no part of life that does not contain lessons. If you are alive, there are lessons to be learned.

6. There is no better place than *here*. When your *there* has become a *here*, you simply will contain another *there* that will again look better than *here*.

7. Others are merely mirrors of you. You cannot love or hate something about another person unless it reflects to you something you love or hate about yourself.

8. What you make of your life is up to you. You have all the tools and resources you need. What you do with them is up to you. The choice is yours.

9. The answers lie inside you. The answers to life's questions lie inside you. All you need to do is look, listen, and trust.

10. You will forget this.

Security is mostly a superstition. It does not exist in nature nor do the children of men as a whole experience it. Avoiding danger is no safer in the long run than outright exposure. Life is either a daring adventure or nothing.

Helen Keller,
American author and lecturer,
deaf and blind
from the age of 18 months.

A Day In The Life of The Resigned
Dr. Joe Rubino

After all is said and done
And today is just a memory
We will look and laugh
And nod and sigh
And think it strange
To have tossed and worried
Hoped and prayed
For so familiar an ending.

Morning dawns
The city rises
Sweeping out the cobwebs of the mind
With well-worn brooms.
The moans of children off to school
To learn the ways to wipe the smiles off their faces.

Along the windings of the streets
The memories strive to linger.
Of those who stood in fear
In stagnant and decaying lives
Not knowing of their right to choose
But opting to malinger.

The midday sun is strong and bright
For those who seek to find the light.
But to those in their hiding places
The darkness tends to conceal all faces.

The sun goes down
As dusk grows near
Turning memory into fear.
The chance to do — again gone by
We turn ...and climb the stair... and sigh.

Too long a day
(He'll turn and say).
She yawns
And nods her head.

Evening's come
The moon reminds
With such a grin
That wipes the laughter from your chin.
The choice to act again passed by.

Bed awaits
It's time for sleep
To gather strength
To live again
The memories that we keep.

CONTENTS

I. Introduction

II. Impacting Your Life and Your Effectiveness

III. Being The Best You Can Be: Accessing Your Personal Power

ACKNOWLEDGMENT

There are so many people I wish to thank who have contributed to both my own personal development as well as to making this book possible.

First, my gratitude goes to Mike and Tinka Smith of BridgeQuest, Carol McCall of The World Institute Group and Richard Brooke, author of *Mach II With Your Hair on Fire*. These mentors introduced me to the concept of personal development and living a life of choice. This book is based upon their insights concerning human communication and interaction as well as the many important principles that contribute to the conversation around human growth and development. Thanks to each one for inspiring me to play full out in life.

Also, special thanks to my business partner, coach and lifelong friend, Dr. Tom Ventullo, with whom I am partnered to bring this work to the world. Tom shares my commitment to impact others through our two companies, The Center For Personal Reinvention, **http://www.CenterFor PersonalReinvention.com/**, and Visionary International Partnerships.

Thanks to my wife, Janice, for her unending love and support, making this work and my commitment to others possible. Thanks also to my family for their constant love, encouragement and belief in me.

I must also thank the thousands of friends, colleagues and visionary partners who have worked with and alongside us since 1991. It is through their partnership and leadership that thousands of people have been impacted to achieve success in life as they honor their values and pursue their passions.

Thanks to all the friends that have attended our courses and participated in the programs offered by The Center For Personal Reinvention, teaching us more each time.

Thanks also to Evelyn Howell for editing *The Power To Succeed* and to Shawn Mathis and Stan Smith for their efforts with the book's preparation. Thanks to Tom Bellucci for his efforts in book and cover design.

And, of course, thanks to you, the reader, for your participation, feedback and courage to take on the process of personal development, reinventing who you are on a day-by-day basis out of the possibility of who you can be for yourself and others.

I

INTRODUCTION

1

My Story of Personal Development

The principles I discuss in this book are responsible for transforming my life. The resignation I wrote about in the opening poem characterized my days. Like so many others, I sensed that life had become stale. Something was missing, but I couldn't identify what it was. Life was not a daring adventure, but a monotonous routine void of passion and fulfillment. As I've since discovered, there was nothing inherently wrong with my life back then. I was just not showing up for life with the zest that naturally comes from identifying and pursuing values and qualities that are most important. Missing was my taking responsibility for making life work by identifying what was most important to me and going for it.

Over the past ten years, I have taken on the process of personal development in order to incorporate the key principles that follow as part of who I am. With some I have achieved various levels of mastery. With others I remain a self-declared novice. Throughout the process, I have trained myself to ask the perpetual questions, "Who am I being on a moment-to-moment basis that either supports who I choose to be or detracts from it?" and "What is missing that if put into place would allow me to better access my personal power in the world and in my relationships with others?"

My life was not always so clearly focused on these questions. Like many, I was educated traditionally in the arts and sciences. My formal education did not include any possibilities of working on increasing my personal effectiveness. Having been attracted to the sciences at an early age, I decided to pursue a college career with the expectation of entering into the medical profession. Coming from the paradigm that knowledge is power, I decided to become a constant seeker of information. After all, isn't it true that information is the source of one's power?

By overachieving (I had to study around the clock to get the grades I would need to get into dental school) I was able to graduate in the top 5 percent of my class at Boston College, thus ensuring my entry into dental school. So far, getting all the information (knowledge) was apparently paying off.

I entered dental school where the prevailing belief was that in order to truly prepare one for the dental profession, it was necessary to make it as difficult and stressful as humanly possible. Not only was success equated with information, but it logically followed that the more difficult it was to acquire that information, the more prepared one should be to succeed. The constant threat of failing inflicted by those who themselves had survived a similar initiation (apparently giving them the right to pass it on to others) was necessary to make sure we, the students, were "ready" to take our places in this hallowed profession. Sure enough, all of the additional information prepared me to enter the dental profession with the competency needed to carry out my chosen occupation. For the next 12 years, this is exactly what I did.

For a while, practicing dentistry was, in many ways, fulfilling. It provided me with the opportunity to contribute to the health and well-being of my patients. It provided my wife, Janice, and me with a prosperous lifestyle. I was busy. I was successful by most Western standards. After all, dentistry was something I knew I could do well to earn a living.

But something was missing. Life had become less than fulfilling, and I was resigned to the fact that I could do little about it. In fact, I was unaware of my ability to affect any change that would make my life more meaningful. I sensed that there was more to life than the endless array of *shoulds* or obligations that had come to make up the substance of my existence. You know the ones. I should go to work every day. I should be responsible and do those monotonous and unpleasant procedures (like root canals) that I so hated. I should see those often angry and difficult patients that I allowed to invariably ruin my day.

Like so many others, I had confused obligation with responsibility. Not only was I not being responsible for honoring my values and powerfully directing my life forward, but I was totally unaware that I even possessed the ability to do so. *And I was resigned to having no choice.*

Then in 1991, while attending a meeting sponsored by Oxyfresh Worldwide, a company known for developing leaders, I was introduced to three people who were to become my mentors for the next ten years. These people were Carol McCall, Mike Smith and Richard Brooke. With their support, I entered into the process of examining who I was, what was most important to me and what gifts I possessed. I realized that I was not honoring my core values of creativity, contribution, freedom and adventure. It became apparent to me that I was playing small in the world. My dental practice served as a comfortable place to hide. It offered a familiar justification for not pushing the edge of the envelope to be the best I could be.

Please do not misunderstand. Dentistry is a great and necessary profession that provides fulfillment to many practitioners and a public service of tremendous value. It allowed me to earn a nice living at something I knew I could keep doing the rest of my working life. It gave me the ability to dominate my environment while providing insulation from the challenges of the outside world. However, the cost of this safety net was my vitality and ability to grow. The cost was most obvious in my relationships, most of which were based on competition and were not very satisfying. Also, playing small hindered my potential to impact and contribute to the lives of others.

It was not until these costs became painfully clear that I was able to garner the necessary self-motivation required to do whatever it would take to break out of my rut. With this realization, I decided to sell my dental practice, put myself into the process of never ending personal development and risk the neat little package of who I was for the possibility of who I might become.

Today, my commitment is to champion others to kill that same resignation that once dominated my own life. I acknowledge those of you who have courageously committed to take on the life-changing path of personal development in pursuit of being all you can be. It is only by maximizing your own personal effectiveness that you will be able to translate this personal power to impact others. It is through this geometrically progressing series of individual personal transformations that a significant global transformation will result.

2

What lies behind us and what lies before us are tiny matters compared to what lies within us.

Oliver Wendell Holmes,
19th-century American poet and novelist

Living in Reaction to Life or Adapting Life to Meet Your Wildest Expectations

Does any of the following describe you?

• Do you often find yourself automatically reacting to people and events? ✓

• Are you constantly at the mercy of circumstances?

• Do you tend to live reactively?

• Are you disconnected and separate from others? Do you see them in competition with you for things you need in order to survive and prosper? ✓

• Is your sense of being disconnected magnified by the false facade you put on to protect yourself? Does your facade keep people out and prevent them from seeing your flaws and weaknesses?

• Do you dismiss thoughts, people or actions that do not fit in with the way you've decided things should be?

• Do you live in the past with the residue from numerous daily incompletions you can't seem to forget about?

• Do you step over problems and emotions to avoid confronting the reality that your life is not working optimally?

• Are you resigned to living a life that does not fully support your magnificence because you have decided that it is impossible or at least too difficult to do anything about it? no

• Do you protect yourself by creating stories to explain, justify or conceal why you do what you do? no

• When you encounter people who oppose you in any way, do you take them out by undermining their credibility with others through gossiping and exaggerating their weaknesses?

• Do you find that your behaviors, interpretations and actions do not support you to be the best you can be?

The above shortcomings characterize those who see the world as a dangerous place marked by scarcity and competition. Contrast them with what is possible.

You can decide to reinvent yourself as follows:

- To live your life as a daring adventure with a commitment to be your best.

- To champion the excellence of others by making unreasonable requests that stretch them to live full out.

- To do the same with respect to yourself.

- To choose to invent your future as a daily creation, reflecting your ability to be both the architect and builder of who you are and who you choose to become.

- To experience each day with the satisfaction that comes from knowing you have lived from your vision for what is possible, not just what is tolerated.

- To proactively live out of a commitment to whole thinking — having life work optimally for you, for others and for the world in general. Not win/lose, either/or, but win/win/win, and/both.

- To connect with others, seeking mutuality whenever possible because what supports one of us, supports us all. We are all connected at some level.

- To live life constantly looking for new ideas with an emphasis on possibility thinking, believing that you can be the source of possibilities showing up in your life.

- To see life as an endless series of opportunities awaiting exploration with nothing but abundance and possibilities to act upon.

● To live with a conscious awareness of your ability to contribute to yourself and to others; the more you give to others, the more you get back in return.

● To be complete with your past, able to fully experience the present and invent your future out of choice.

● To get feedback from others and have life train you by providing continual input allowing you to benefit the most from what you learn.

● To acknowledge your accomplishments and savor your growth and daily victories before refocusing your sights on what is next.

In short, life can either be an uphill struggle that looks like something you have to survive or it can be a daring adventure played full out in partnership with others. You get to choose which it will be.

This book and its sequel, *The Power to Succeed: More Principles for Powerful Living, Book II,* will address each of the above challenges and potentialities. Together we will explore in life-changing detail just what it might look like to reinvent who you are with the intention of maximizing your personal power, productivity, effectiveness and happiness.

3

*D*evelop wisdom, good judgment and common sense. This will
protect you.

Proverbs 4:5

Assimilating Key Principles

In our culture, we mistakenly live the interpretation that
information is the source of people being effective and
powerful. People go to schools for years to acquire enough
information on how to do something with the hope and
expectation that the information will lead to their success in
life. However, while valuable, information alone is not the
source of action or of being effective and powerful in the
world. If it were, those with the most education would always
be the most successful. Likewise, experience alone does not
guarantee effectiveness. If it did, those most powerful would
always be those who had been doing something for the longest
time. We know that this is often not the case.

True power and effectiveness come as a result of developing key principles — as opposed to just acquiring information

or experience. You cannot fully experience those things for which you have not developed the necessary foundational principles. For the purpose of this book, we'll call these foundational principles "distinctions." In other words, there is a major difference between conceptualizing or knowing what to do, doing it, and actually *getting* it. In fact, the best way to develop a particular principle or distinction is to actually acquire it in the process of failing while pursuing it. Gaining a principle will come from actually engaging in a state of inquiry with an attitude that it's perfectly all right to be awkward and even fall on your face as you explore new and uncharted territory.

As an example, learning to ride a bike is a function of the distinction balance. It is not directly related to any information you might gather about riding the bike. Although you could read every book ever written on bicycles and riding them, the only way you'll ever learn to actually succeed in riding a bike is by going through the actual process until you get what balance is all about. Before you learn to ride, before you get what balance is and what having balance feels like, you are likely to fail many times. Gaining the principle of balance will only result through persevering — hanging in there, falling off the bike, wobbling from side to side and continually getting back on the bike for as long as it takes before you actually acquire balance. Until you have balance, you cannot experience riding the bike.

Your effectiveness in any arena of life is a function of the key principles and skills you have. Beyond information, beyond experience, these principles are about being. You actually acquire the principle as it becomes a part of who you are. People that are gifted in a particular area have an inherent grasp of principles that others do not. Once you get one of these principles, it must continually be recreated in order to access the power in it. But even if it is not regularly used or if is largely forgotten, once you have it, it's never lost. It will become more powerful as you use it, recreating it over and over again through action and communication.

The skilled surgeon has acquired and integrated skills and principles that medical students do not have yet. Dentists likewise notice details in the mouth that non-dentists cannot because they possess the appropriate distinctions. Eskimos have more than 25 different terms for snow based upon the various properties different snows possess. Some snows can be used to build igloos, other snows cause avalanches, still others indicate weather changes to come, and so forth. Eskimos are skilled in the arena of snow because they have the foundational principles that most of us do not.

The principles we explore are about the study of *being*. The question you will continually be asked to examine is, "Who are you being that either causes you to access your power and have your life and relationships with others work optimally — or not?"

The principles I discuss are by necessity of the written word presented as information, and information alone cannot suffice if you are to truly acquire these principles as powerful, life-changing distinctions. Principles must be created and then acquired to make a difference for your life to work. With some, you will acquire them easily. With others, your willingness to be uncomfortable and hang in there will determine your ultimate success. Getting a key principle or distinction is an all-at-once phenomenon; once you really get it, you never lose it. It' yours for life. Ultimately, what allows something to show up for you is the distinction you have for it.

As a result, with each principle, I also present exercises designed to support you in developing these principles so they become part of your very being.

If putting yourself in development with the intention of reinventing who you are is an appealing concept, I encourage you to take on a rigorous program that would support you in this goal. In addition to our own Center For Personal

Reinvention, **http://www.CenterForPersonalReinvention. com**, extraordinary programs are offered by Carol McCall, Mike and Tinka Smith and Richard and Rishon Brooke. McCall is the world's foremost expert in the technology of listening. The Smiths are masterful in leadership development and the Brookes are known for their work on vision and self-motivation. Short of your becoming involved with such a program, the only way I know for the principles presented to come alive for you is to actually do the exercises presented in this book and its sequel, *The Power To Succeed: More Principles for Powerful Living — Book II.*

I acknowledge you for taking on this journey of personal expansion. This book is dedicated to those of you who have chosen to follow the path of heart in constant search of being the very best you can be, improving with each passing day. May your life be filled with the principles that provide you with happiness, rich relationships and personal power.

II

IMPACTING YOUR LIFE AND YOUR EFFECTIVENESS

—————————— **4** ——————————

Growth depends on being always in motion just a little bit, one way or another.

Norman Mailer,
American author

Creating a Structure for Getting the Most Out of This Book

In order to get the most out of this work, it is essential that you actually experience the principles presented. The ideal way to do this would be to hire one or more coaches to support you in gaining insight into those areas that are outside of your customary way of viewing the world and acting upon its challenges. Your coaches should be individuals who themselves possess the key principles that make them powerful in the particular arena they offer coaching. A coach may be powerful in some arenas but not necessarily in others. The same person who is qualified to coach you in business matters may be totally unqualified to coach you in the area of relationships or spiritual matters. True coaches do not give advice or lend their opinions. They are value based, not ego based. They do not manipulate or exploit to carry out their own agenda. They are not the same as counselors or therapists. They do not try to protect, control or rescue those they are coaching. They instead listen for where one may be experiencing challenges or may be missing some key element that, if put into place, would impact a desired result. Coaches support us in seeing something that we may not be aware of by listening both to what we say and to what we leave out. They have empathy for the person being coached but are not emotionally attached to an outcome. They serve to champion people to have their lives work optimally. They do this by asking questions, exploring possibilities, making requests and, at times, confronting issues that may need to be examined. Skilled coaching is a fine art and a highly valuable service.

Another way to fully experience the principles presented would be to enter into a structured personal development program like those offered by The Center For Personal Reinvention, BridgeQuest, The World Institute Group or any number of other excellent programs available. Over the course of several years, as you adopt the principles as part of your daily life, they will eventually become part and parcel of your very being. Unfortunately, these approaches are not always practical for everyone.

A good alternative is to get together with one to five other people who have an interest in increasing their personal effectiveness. Request that everyone read through this entire book first. Then commit to supporting each other to fully explore, digest, discuss and experience each principle one at a time, one each week. As a group, create an alternating schedule for each person to take a turn leading the discussion around each concept presented. Read each principle together. Discuss with each other any insights, questions or challenges each one brings up for the group.

For the week that follows, immerse yourself in the principle presented. Thoroughly explore the questions offered at the end of each principle covered. Look for any revelations around where you might increase your personal power and effectiveness. Search for any interpretations or behaviors that do not support your excellence and your relationships with others.

At the end of the week, get together with those in the group either in person or by telephone and share what you learned. Discuss any insights or breakthroughs you gained by putting yourself in the work. Rate your level of engagement on a scale from 1 to 10 and discuss any obstacles that may be limiting your participation or effectiveness.

As each week progresses, keep in front of you those principles you've explored in prior weeks as you take on each new concept. Do you see any patterns developing? Request and remain open to feedback from other members of the group, inviting each other's insights. Often, although we can clearly see where others are stopped in life, we are the last to recognize our own limitations.

The principles we will explore together are presented from the perspective that mastery of the various concepts and exercises will support anyone in better accessing their personal power to be the very best they can be. The concepts discussed are not being presented as *the truth*. Truth is an interpretation and as such is a relative term. What is true for one person may not be true for another.

It is extremely important that you do the suggested exercises. Without experiencing the principles discussed so as to actually acquire them, the next pages will seem like just interesting ideas. To impact your life, live the principles until they become part of your being. Your commitment to do so will directly impact your personal power.

Do each exercise for at least a week or for as long as is necessary to master the concepts presented. You may want to go on to subsequent principles as you see progress with the ones you have taken on. Do as many simultaneously as you can manage. It is essential to continuously revisit those principles you have developed from time to time. Once you truly acquire a principle, you never lose it. At the same time, each area is never handled. Without a commitment to keep immersed in the work of personal development, it's too easy to fall back into old habits.

Keep a journal. Any spiral-bound notebook will do. Record your observations, challenges, insights and progress. Your development will progress consistent with your willingness to keep the appropriate questions before you. After each day, conduct a debriefing session with yourself. Answer the questions presented, reflect on the exercises and record your observations. Always ask yourself, "What worked about my interactions with others?" and "What was missing that if put into place would make me more effective?"

And lastly, by all means have fun. Don't take yourself too seriously. Loosen up, relax and make the process of personal development an enjoyable one. Your willingness to laugh at yourself and enjoy the personal development experience will be a key factor that contributes to your success.

5

T rue belonging is born of relationships not only to one another but to a place of shared responsibilities and benefits.

Robert Finch,
U.S. Secretary of Health,
Education and Welfare, 1969-70

Creating an Environment for Maximizing Your Power

J oan lives in the poor part of town. Although she always dreamed of living in a beautiful house in the country, her husband's modest paycheck does not allow them to live anywhere but in the inner city. Her 12-year-old Ford Escort is badly dented, rusting and constantly in need of repair. Always struggling to pay her bills, Joan is overweight, has poor dental health and dresses in a manner that reflects her lot in life. Her son Adam is always getting into trouble with his friends, who see drugs and crime as the only way to make enough money to get ahead in life. Joan feels angry that she has been dealt such a tough life, but believes that there is little she can do about it.

Who and what we surround ourselves with has a great deal to do with creating an environment that either champions us to be all we can be or sabotages us in this effort. Do the people and elements in your daily life support those values that are most important to you? Do they inspire you with similar values or bring you down? Are your home and office healthy and conducive to your happiness and growth? Or are your surroundings filled with things that don't support your excellence? Do your health, appearance and lifestyle support the person you choose to be or detract from it? Are you living in harmony with your values and designing your future or are you at the mercy of whatever problems confront you daily? Do you live in the area and climate of your choosing, surrounding yourself with plants and animals that contribute to the quality of your life? Are your dress, home, car and possessions a manifestation of your excellence? Is your free time spent in pursuits that bring you closer to the person you choose to be or do you squander your time with mindless diversions?

In the end, every day that you live, you are either experiencing by choice or you are a victim of your environment, helpless to set your own destiny. You are either living out of your values or are at the whims of your ego. You are needy or you are the source of everything that shows up around you.

YOU GET TO CHOOSE.

YOU HAVE THE POWER TO DO SO.

Designing an Environment to Support Who You Choose to Be

1) Do the people, surroundings and circumstances in your life fully support your excellence?

2) Decide today to design your life out of total choice. Examine the following areas to see if each fully meets your needs and expectations:

Family and relationships

Occupation

Physical environment

Recreation, hobbies and passions

Spirituality

3) With the support of a coach or your discussion group, develop a detailed action plan in each area you will redesign. Ask yourself the following questions with respect to each area:

• Do the current conditions of your life support the person you have decided to be?

• What is working and not working about each one?

• What elements are missing that, if put into place, would enhance the quality of each area? Be specific.

• Where is bold action and drastic change required? What bold actions are necessary to directly address any inadequate areas?

- Who will you request to support or coach you in each area you seek to impact?
- By when will you take action?

4) Record your answers to the above questions in your journal.

6

*G*enius is the talent for seeing things straight.

Maude Adams,
American actress best known for her portrayal
of Peter Pan in that 1905 play

Influencing Results in Life by Developing Key Principles

Most of us want to be more effective at everything we do. So how can we best get the results we want? The secret lies in examining how we perceive the world around us.

When we wish to affect a situation's outcome, we typically focus on our actions. We look for what we can do to bring about the results we desire. If we change our actions, we expect to see a change in results in a typical cause-and-effect relationship. But it goes well beyond this.

We must also take into consideration what influences our actions. Because we act according to how we see the world, it makes sense that if we can influence how things appear to us,

43

our actions will respond accordingly. So, how do we influence the way we see things?

We see things first as mental images we create for ourselves. We evaluate these images and then automatically take actions to deal with the perceived situation. So if we can shift the images in our mind, we will come up with different interpretations that will lead to different actions and different results. The secret then is to work on generating images that support us, those that produce actions leading to results consistent with our excellence.

So, what determines the images of how we perceive the world? The answer lies in the foundational principles we possess. We only see those things for which we possess a distinct awareness. As an elementary example, take a drive through the country on a familiar rural residential road — and look for telephone poles. Although you may have driven on that same road a hundred times before, chances are, you never even noticed the poles. This time, because you focus on the poles, they will likely show up like never before.

If you can gain the principles necessary to live a powerful life that fully supports you, you will see things differently and therefore act differently. All of our past experiences combine to influence how we see and evaluate everything. Our experiences effectively result in the formation of a filter through which we see all future happenings. The images we create and recreate are consistent with the filter through which we view the world. As we act in accordance with what we perceive through our filter, we produce results consistent with our filtered perceptions. This serves to further strengthen the filter, which in turn produces more of the same results. And on and on it goes. How we see things determines what our actions will be, which, in turn, impacts the results we get.

Consider that you have a pair of sunglasses with red-colored lenses. When you look out at the world, everything you see has a red tint. Imagine that each time you view an object, a sensor in your sunglasses recognizes that the object has a red tint and automatically makes your red lenses one shade darker. The more you look through your red-colored lenses, the redder the world appears.

The same principle applies to our experiences. For example, Bob's father beat him when Bob was a boy. His interpretation of his experiences taught Bob that the world is a harsh and angry place. He learned that to survive, you must be tough and ruthless. Because he sees the world this way, Bob lies, fights and gets into endless trouble. This only serves to reinforce his mental image of the world as a dog-eat-dog place.

Each of Bob's experiences reinforces this image. The result is a downward spiral of interpretations and actions that do not support his happiness and effectiveness with others.

If we can alter the filtered lens through which we view life, we will alter our actions and impact what shows up around us. To shift this filter, first be aware of the basic perceptions that influence how you receive life. What are your automatic assumptions that color how you see the circumstances and relationships around you? What subliminal messages do you send yourself during every conversation, every interaction of your day? Don't despair if it seems like a struggle to notice them. Developing this awareness takes time. Your filter started forming in infancy and is designed to run "invisibly" in the background, like the operating system of a computer.

This book will focus upon a number of key principles that can alter your filtered lens. You will begin to see life differently. By developing the principles necessary to empower you in your day-to-day life, you will have the opportunity to increase your personal power and effectiveness in all you do.

To be truly powerful in life, it is necessary to be effective in each of the following arenas:

- Physical, Mental, and Spiritual Health
- Relationships
- Career
- Finances
- Recreation and Passions
- Personal Development

Developing the key principles in each realm will ensure that we maximize our personal power. Our willingness to play at risk, expanding ourselves beyond our comfort zones, will determine the extent of the personal development we reach.

In order to protect ourselves from any negative consequences we might experience as a result of venturing beyond our comfort zone, it is prudent to maintain a reserve. When you have a reserve in each of these areas, you can better deal with any challenges or setbacks you may experience. Maintaining this reserve will allow you to draw upon that extra energy and support as you deal with any of the challenges that life sends your way. You will find yourself more at peace without the need to mentally deal with the many concerns that keep you from enjoying life. Coming from the state of being centered and ready for whatever surprises life has to offer, you can be proactive rather than reactive. You can now operate from strength instead of being on edge, in a survival mode. This will allow you to integrate power into all areas of your life.

Impacting the Areas of Your Life

1) Take an inventory of each of the following key areas of your life:

- Physical, Mental and Spiritual Health
- Relationships
- Career
- Finances
- Recreation and Passions
- Personal Growth and Development

2) Now, for each area of your life, identify:

- Those areas where you are currently most powerful.
- Those areas you have decided to take on next in your personal development.
- Who you will hire to coach you in each of these areas.
- Those areas where you will develop more of a reserve to afford you the protection you'll need to play full out.
- Any stops to claiming your power in each area.

III

BEING THE BEST YOU CAN BE:

ACCESSING YOUR PERSONAL POWER

———————————— **7** ————————————

I know of no more encouraging fact than the unquestionable
ability of man to elevate his life by conscious endeavor.

Henry David Thoreau,
19th-century American essayist and poet

Selecting Areas for Personal Development and Evaluating Your Progress on a Regular Basis

As human beings, we are in a constant state of flux —
physically, emotionally, mentally and spiritually. Life
presents us with never-ending opportunities to put ourselves
into personal development. What we do with each of these
opportunities is entirely up to us. Daily, we are offered a
choice. We can respond to life's challenges by either resisting
or embracing them. Taking the path of personal development
means examining who we are today and who we choose to be
tomorrow, all the while evaluating how we are doing along the

way. If we are not climbing the mountain of self-improvement, then we are sliding down the hill of decay. There is no standing still.

The decision to make each day an opportunity for personal development means committing to continual and never ending improvement in some aspect of our lives. In order to support this commitment, it is helpful to implement a structure to examine what's going on in our world. This structure must involve a means to get feedback on what is working, what is not working and what is now missing that, if put into place, will take us to the next level.

Some possible areas of personal development might involve working on any of the following qualities:

- Being calm and centered
- Not reacting
- Being organized and focused
- Being at peace
- Having genuine humility
- Choosing interpretations that support or empower you
- Having greater physical energy
- Working on your health and appearance
- Having integrity
- Exuding charisma

- Showing confidence
- Being an inspiration to yourself and others
- Allowing yourself to be vulnerable
- Showing emotion
- Not showing emotion when it does not serve you
- Being sensitive
- Being consistent or persistent
- Being coachable or teachable
- Being happy
- Having a good self-image
- Trusting your intuition
- Developing empathy
- Being self-motivated
- Being able to make and keep commitments
- Being able to be told anything without reacting
- Being a good listener
- Being able to make the most of any situation
- Being able to have fun
- Coming across authentically to others
- Having discipline
- Willing to sacrifice for the future
- Speaking from the heart
- Living your vision
- Supporting others

- Championing others to excellence
- Exuding enthusiasm
- Being inspirational
- Being vulnerable
- Having compassion
- Possessing a positive attitude
- Choosing to have positive expectations
- Communicating effectively

You might choose to develop the following qualities in relation to others:

- Developing an empathic awareness of what it's like to be in the other person's situation
- Listening for how to contribute to or support others
- Listening for mutuality or common ground
- Listening for what others have to contribute to you
- Being able to bond with others
- Possessing the ability to work well in partnership
- Being happy to serve
- Being willing to contribute
- Being interested in others
- Being interested in finding solutions that work for everyone
- Not interrupting

- Being able to impact people positively
- Being a team player

To enhance your personal power, create a structure to develop whatever qualities you decide to take on. Some possible structures include:

- Hiring a mentor to coach you to put into place those missing qualities you seek to develop.

- Rating yourself after each interaction (on a scale from 1 to 10) as to how successful you were in implementing the quality you're working on. Look at what worked, what was missing and what you need to put into place the next time to be more effective in the area you are developing.

- Keeping a journal detailing your daily, intended result in your chosen area of development. Again, record both what worked and what was missing.

- Asking others for feedback. You might say something like, "I am working on the quality of becoming more charismatic, a better listener, more powerful in my communication, etc. Could you give me some feedback on how I came across for you?"

Your commitment to research which qualities would most impact who you are and your willingness to create a structure to support this commitment will do much toward increasing your personal power.

Creating a Structure to Support Your Development

1) Make a list of all of the qualities you like and dislike about yourself.

2) List at least five qualities you would be willing to develop further.

3) Select a structure to support you in developing these qualities, such as:

- Working with a coach or mentor
- Rating yourself after each interaction you have
- Recording your observations in your journal
- Requesting feedback from others

Evaluating Your Personal Development

1) At the end of each day, each week and each month ask yourself the following questions to gauge how you did in your areas of personal development:

- What did you learn about yourself and others?
- In what ways were you effective in your interactions?

- What was missing that, if put in place, would make you more effective?

2) Record your insights in your journal.

8

We are what we repeatedly do. Excellence, then, is not an act but a habit.

Aristotle,
Ancient Greek philosopher and
author of works on logic, philosophy, ethics, politics
and natural science

The Elements of Accomplishment

There are three distinct elements to consider in putting yourself on the path of enhanced productivity and continual self-improvement. Any time you take on a new goal, you will want to look at these three elements before you declare yourself fully successful.

1- You must produce a result.

With any endeavor that involves a goal or accomplishment, there needs to be a measurable result. Without some discernible accomplishment, the element of productivity is lacking. Notice whenever you either produce a result or have some story, justification or excuse for why the result may be lacking. Your power will come from taking responsibility for making a result happen in spite of any challenges or circumstances that may cross your path.

2- There must be personal development occurring.
You can achieve all the money, possessions and fame possible, but without learning something that moves you forward personally, the achievement is incomplete. Your intention to examine each situation, interaction and communication to evaluate what worked about it and what was missing that may have supported your power and effectiveness will provide insights to ensure that this element of personal development is present as you go about your day.

3- You must have fun.
No matter how successful you may be, if you hate the process and have not stopped to enjoy yourself along the way, your accomplishment has surely been lacking. You get to decide what will constitute having fun. Identify your values and passions and ensure that they are honored and included as a condition that must be met as you design your accomplishments. Your focus on having fun will result in it happening because of your intention that it be so.

Rating Your Accomplishments

As you take on projects and set goals, rate yourself on a scale from 1 to 10 in your journal with respect to:

    A- Measurable Results

    B- Personal Growth

    C- Fun

Your focus on all three areas will produce a worthwhile and enjoyable victory with substance.

———————— **9** ————————

One finds one's way only by taking it.

William Clark,
18th-century explorer of the American West,
the Lewis and Clark Expedition

Responsibility

"**I**t weren't my fault. Were it?" was the comical phrase often repeated by the old cowboy that actor Walter Brennan played in one of his classic movies. We often hold this same perspective. All the unfortunate occurrences, problematic relationships and daily challenges that come our way couldn't possibly be our fault. It's usually the other guy or the circumstances that are really to blame. We see responsibility as something to avoid, and this view does not serve us well.

Responsibility is actually the ability to respond at any time and to any situation in a way that honors you as a person and supports you in your relationships with others. Contrast this with how we have been trained to view responsibility.

Responsibility does not involve blame, fault or burden. Not being responsible does not connote shame, guilt or unworthiness. It does not involve a value judgment subject to someone's opinion about how you *should* do something or how someone ought to run his or her life. Responsibility instead involves taking full acceptance for every event, relationship, action and situation that occurs in your life. It is not actually *true* that you bring about everything that shows up around you. It is merely an interpretation or tool that I suggest you use: that everything you do, whatever you have and how you show up for others is your creation. This posture is one you can take to empower you to be the source of what happens to you. Being responsible means that there are no victims created by life's events. In some way, consciously or not, every person, circumstance, event or challenge we encounter in life is the result of decisions we have made.

This is not to say that events do not occur that are outside of the scope of our influence. Such situations certainly do take place. To say that we are responsible for everything that happens around us is simply a declaration that reminds us to be aware that we make the choices and decisions of our lives. It is a place we stand as we invoke our personal power to choose.

63

Responsibility is always in the present, never about the past. It is a place to stand to look at the world as you make a choice about some action you may take. It does not make anyone wrong or at fault, and it does not involve manipulation. When any situation touches our lives, taking responsibility means we take the interpretation that it simply *occurred* as opposed to the interpretation that it happened *to* us. Having responsibility implies that you are the designer and builder of who you are, what you have and what you do. And, since it's your creation, you get to change it if what you see around you is not to your liking.

Taking responsibility means giving up your "right" to make others wrong. It is about saying what you need to say without harboring ill feelings, resentment or getting back at the person in some way. People who take responsibility are empowered to respond to any situation with a self-assured, personal power and knowledge that they can affect change.

Remember, you are the source for what you attract in the world. Claim responsibility for everything in your life and decide to take the necessary steps to impact what shows up around you.

Living Responsibly

1) In the areas of your health, relationships, finances and career, identify where you have been less than responsible.

2) Taking total responsibility, what actions will you take to design what your life will look like in each of these areas? What deadline will you set for taking these actions?

3) Record your insights and commitments in your journal.

10

No one can hurt you without your consent.

Eleanor Roosevelt,
American diplomat, writer, humanitarian and
First Lady, 1933-45

There Is No Such Thing As a Failure!

Does this ever describe you? The mere possibility of failing at an endeavor is so frightening that you are reluctant to take on a challenge just so you avoid any *chance* of failing. This happens when you become so attached to an outcome that you have no room to maneuver successfully in order to succeed. If you have no room to fail, you also have no room to succeed.

Remember, failure is an interpretation — not a fact. Do you know who was the greatest baseball strikeout king of all time? Babe Ruth. Yes, the Babe struck out more times than anyone else. He was also the number one homerun king for decades as well. Failure or tremendous success? It all depends on your focus and your interpretation.

The same is true of inventor Thomas Edison. Before he invented the electric light bulb, he *failed* at his 400-plus prior attempts. When asked about all these apparent failures, Edison responded that they were not failures at all. In fact, he had successfully discovered more than 400 ways that were not the answer to generating indoor lighting.

We tend to look for the flaw in whatever we do and find countless ways to invalidate ourselves. We zoom in on our shortcomings instead of focusing on our accomplishments. The inability to accept our failures as valid actually limits our actions. If we cannot experience setbacks, we do not allow ourselves the room to experiment beyond the limits of our knowledge.

When you give yourself the room to experience new challenges, to learn from these experiences and to grow from the wisdom they provide, you are to be acknowledged just for putting out the effort. Your courage to attempt the unknown will create countless opportunities for discoveries into realms previously unexplored.

To become empowered to venture into uncharted waters, declare yourself a novice in these areas. Exploring the unknown with open curiosity and without an attachment to a particular result creates the space for new experiences and potential successes.

Another way to approach a concern about failing at your goals is to take your focus off the result. When obsessed with achieving an elusive desired objective, we may become so frustrated that our effectiveness suffers. As a result, we drift farther from the very thing we want most.

You can still be committed to a result without being attached to it. Place your attention on the actions required to obtain your intended result. By concentrating on your game plan, you can evaluate your progress, see what's working and what's missing and alter your actions to better put into place what is needed to come in on target. Much of that information and discovery would be limited were it not for the successful revelation of failure.

One last thought about failure. Most people are scared to death to fail. If this describes you, lighten up. Don't take failure too seriously. So what if you fail? Go ahead and play full out. If you create a bunch of failures, embrace them. Don't run from failure. Once you get that it's all right to fail, you can become empowered by creating so much failure that it will become an unimportant condition. Give yourself the room to play all out and fail if necessary. Doing so also creates the room to do what it takes to succeed. In the end, your satisfaction will come from doing your very best, free from your fear of failing, no matter what the outcome.

Embracing Failure, Eliminating the Fear

1) Where have you not attempted something for fear of failing?

2) What empowering interpretation can you create to take the place of fearing that you may fail?

3) Design a detailed action plan to achieve an objective that you have been reluctant to take on. How does your plan incorporate failure to benefit your momentum?

4) Record your observations and insights in your journal.

11

Happiness is not a goal, it's a byproduct.

Eleanor Roosevelt

Are You Living Life Backwards?

*arry was a tremendous success by most standards. He had
built a company from scratch that netted $5 million a year in
bottom-line profit. He had all the houses, cars, boats and other toys
that we usually equate with success. But no matter how well he did,
no matter how much wealth or how many things he amassed, it was
never quite enough. He somehow could not get over the persistent
thought that he was a failure. There was little satisfaction in anything he accomplished. Throughout his childhood, if his report card
showed all A's and a B+, he would be disappointed for not applying
himself more. He could still hear his dad scolding him, saying,
"Come on, Larry! You can do better than that!"*

It was the same story for everything he did. No matter what the accomplishment, the feeling of satisfaction was always short-lived. He would always find a way to invalidate himself, thinking it wasn't that big a deal after all to achieve whatever he did. There was always another bigger, steeper, tougher mountain to climb. Once he climbed THAT mountain, he'd be happy. But after doing so, there was always little sense of lasting accomplishment awaiting him at the top. So, he'd be off looking for that next prize to attain — and then, surely, he'd be happy.

In our quest to provide ourselves with evidence to support our identity and our actions, we typically live life backwards. We feel like we must first *HAVE* in order to *DO* in order to *BE*.

We strive to HAVE knowledge, possessions and wealth so that we might be able to DO those things that are important to us, like spending time with those we love and pursuing our hobbies and passions, in order to BE or become the type of person that fits with the image we would like for ourselves.

This illogical and reversed approach to life comes from our need to amass evidence to support who we say we are. With enough evidence we think we justify who we claim to be. This logic keeps us from ever achieving satisfaction and fulfillment because we can always find enough evidence to convince us that we have not achieved enough and that we are never good enough to be who we want to be. This approach has us driven, always *doing* and never getting to be.

In contrast to this flow of needing *to have-to do-to be,* instead consider living from a declaration describing who you have decided to be. This is an existential act of courage that allows you to proclaim who you are without needing any evidence to support it. It looks like *being* who you decide to be out of your stating so while *doing* the actions that are appropriate for the person you have affirmed yourself to be.

As a result of who you are and what you do, you'll naturally *have* those qualities and things that provide you with a rich sense of satisfaction and fulfillment. Your life flows out of your declaration. No evidence is required. You are empowered to act because of who you are and your actions will cause you to have those things consistent with who you are and what you do.

Living Life Out of Your Declaration of Who You Choose to Be

1) In the different areas of your life, where do you need evidence to be the person you want to be?

2) From what newly invented declaration will you choose to live? In other words, who will you be? Speak this as an empowering affirmation, "I am a …"

3) What actions are consistent with this declaration?

4) Record your invented declaration in your journal, listing all of the qualities you will be known for as well as the actions you will commit to that are consistent with this declaration.

12

We can be absolutely certain only about things we do not understand.

Eric Hoffer,
20th-century American social philosopher,
writer, and longshoreman

It is the tragedy of the world that no one knows what he doesn't know — and the less a man knows, the more sure he is that he knows everything.

Joyce Cary,
American author

Being Committed to the Question More Than the Answer

There was once a very wealthy and learned young man who went to the East to seek out a wise Zen master as his new mentor. He joined him for afternoon tea saying, "Wise Master, I have studied at many universities and obtained many degrees and have been subjected to many foolish people who have been able to teach me little that I have not already known. I now wish to study with you so that you can teach me all your wisdom."

The Zen master reached over to pour tea into the young man's tea cup. The hot tea filled the cup and continued to flow out all over the young man's clothes, burning him in the process. The young man jumped up and yelled, "You stupid old man, can't you see what you are doing? You're spilling hot tea all over me!"

The Zen master stopped pouring and spoke, "Young man, until your cup is empty, you are incapable of receiving anything from me. Go now and return when you are able to make room to receive from another."

In our western culture, we are addicted to finding the answer. No matter what the question is, we look for The Answer that will solve our problem. Our addiction to The Answer keeps us from the much more valuable practice of discovering what is possible. In contrast to needing to come up with the answer to any concern, a willingness to remain always open and curious will provide us with a rich, continuing flow of insights leading to a more profound understanding.

Impatience in staying with the question often comes from an unwillingness to admit that we do not have all the answers.

Declaring ourselves novices in any arena creates room to adequately investigate all of the possibilities and ramifications without having to come up with an answer. It is often more productive to generate possibilities than to rush into finding a solution or answer that, once found, shuts off any further exploration of the question.

Staying With the Question

Begin to notice any attachment to finding the answer to a problem. Decide instead to stay open to possibilities and to keep inquiring. Write your daily observations in your journal.

"Until you empty your cup to create room to receive from others, all contributions will be wasted."

13

*E*ach forward step we take we leave some phantom of ourselves
behind.

John Lancaster Spalding,
American author

Designing Your Future

Tomas was born into a life of poverty and struggle. Like his
parents and grandparents before him, he grew up knowing
that he and his future family would be dependent on the public welfare system for their survival. "That's just the way it is," Tomas
laments. "Everyone knows that you're born into this life of poverty
and there's no escaping it. To think there's a way out is just to refuse
to face reality."

Shirley grew up in a middle-class household. Her goal in life
was to meet a nice guy, get married and settle down to raise a
family. When she was 17, Shirley got pregnant and was obliged to
marry a man she neither loved nor respected. Despite the fact that
she and her husband had little in common and were not together by

77

choice, they saw their relationship as a necessary duty and obligation. Life was, therefore, one of quiet desperation.

Everyone in Dan's family worked as a union member for the local steel industry. From the earliest age he could remember, Dan knew that it was expected that one day, he, too, would follow in his father's and his grandfather's footsteps and become a member of the local union chapter. As Dan grew up, he developed a love of nature and the outdoors. To Dan, the ideal occupation would be one where he could work in the wilderness among the trees and animals. But everyone knew Dan would do as he was expected and join the union, just as his two brothers had done before him. And so, Dan was resigned to this fact.

For most people, the future looks like a mere extension of the past. Their expectation of what is to be is consistent with what has been — with a slight and predictable level of improvement.

In contrast to this, consider the possibility that the future lives as the realization of a promise you make to yourself and to the world. The future will result from your expectations. The quality of your future will be influenced by the commitment you have for it. It lives as a possibility you get to invent.

You are the sole designer and builder of what is to be, and the result will be entirely consistent with your expectation.

Richard Brooke, author of *Mach II With Your Hair on Fire,* tells us that our future will be directly related to what we expect it to be. If we expect it to be worse than our current situation in life, we will sabotage ourselves, causing it to turn out in alignment with this self-fulfilling prophesy. If we expect more of the same results we have experienced to date, our apathy will generate a future consistent with this expectation. And lastly, if our expectation is that the future will be better than our present situation, self-motivation will result to bring about the positive outcome we envision.

How our positive or negative expectancy plays out as a self-fulfilling prophesy can be seen in the example of a novice marathon runner who finds himself out in front, leading the pack at the halfway point in the race. If his expectation is to lose the race, self-defeating thoughts like he is not worthy of winning or he has just been lucky to get off to a good start will take over. This expectation will result in him "choking" and being overtaken by another seasoned runner with a more positive expectation.

The same principle applies to the ghetto child who grows up with the expectation that life is about struggle and scarcity.

This expectation will likely blind her to possibilities that a more positive expectation would support.

We get what we expect. Take full responsibility for expecting your future to be the way you want it to turn out. Realize that you have consciously or unconsciously attracted to you everything that shows up in your life. If where you are in life, the relationships you have attracted and your physical, financial, emotional and spiritual states are not what you desire, decide now to alter your course.

1. Change your expectations.
2. Design a game plan for action consistent with your expectations.
3. Make requests of those who can support your efforts in some way.

The future exists for each of us as a possibility. When we train ourselves to first expect positive results and then act in accordance with what we expect, we set the stage for a bright and promising tomorrow. We have the personal power to create our future on purpose out of our expectation. To the extent we take responsibility to expect a positive tomorrow, speak our vision in a way that enrolls others in its possibilities and get into action to bring it about, we will be the force behind its realization.

The Circle of Sabotage

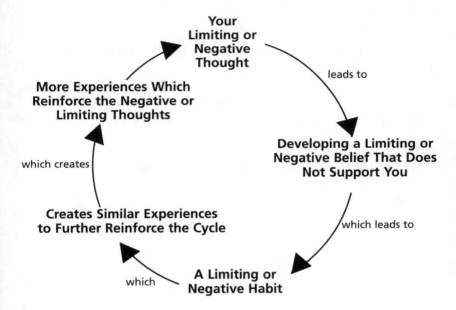

...and the vicious cycle continues, gaining momentum in the wrong direction, taking you further away from the person you want to be.

Exercise for Designing Your Future

1) In your journal, document your expectations for the future in the areas of health, prosperity, relationships and personal growth. Be clear and specify the measurable results you expect.

2) Identify any existing negative expectations that could sabotage your future results and cause you to return to a way of life that does not support your excellence and happiness.

3) What will it cost you to not achieve your expectations? Be specific.

4) Record your observations in your journal.

14

*T*hings that matter most must never be at the mercy of things
that matter least.

Goethe,
18th-century German poet and dramatist

*O*ur values are not luxuries but necessities — not the salt in our
bread but the bread itself — greater than the bounty of all our
material blessings.

Jimmy Carter,
39th U.S. President

Maximizing Your Productivity by Honoring Your Values and Life Rules

*C*reativity and contribution were two of Joe's most important
values. He loved brainstorming new and exciting possibilities
to help people succeed. Joe was most alive when he was utilizing his
creativity to generate new ideas and innovative approaches to any
situation that presented a challenge.

However, not being in touch with this passion, Joe chose a
profession that offered other worthwhile benefits such as financial

security, prestige and safety. For 15 years, as a dentist, Joe practiced his profession dutifully — not realizing what he was missing by ignoring the values of creativity and contribution he so cherished. The result was a sense of something missing and a "Is that all there is to life?" feeling of resignation and burnout.

It was only by focusing on what his values were, identifying which ones were not being honored and becoming aware of what was most important to him that he was able to restructure his priorities and change professions to be more in line with his core values. Today, Joe is championing others to realize their own values, passions and dreams and is thus living his own. The result is that, for Joe, work has become play. As he lives his key values of creativity and contribution, his passion manifests in the world allowing him to access his personal power.

As you may have guessed, Joe's story is my own.

We all have a set of rules we follow which serves as a guide to our lives. For the most part, these rules exist in the background. Although they are often concealed from conscious awareness, they shape our expectations and interactions. If you are denying the importance of your core values and life rules, you may not realize that they are, in fact, your values and rules. They exist nonetheless. Age is not a guarantee of eventual realization, nor should youth be assumed to be an insurmountable obstacle to discovering them. Uncovering and becoming aware of these rules or conditions is essential for us to move deliberately and powerfully forward. By exposing and clarifying what our expectations or life rules are, we become free to examine just how they support or hinder us in our relationships and in achieving our goals. Discovering what your core values are is as simple as looking at the list of values to follow and asking yourself, "What would life be like if this particular value was violated or nonexistent in my life?"

When we violate the life rules based upon our value system, then frustration, anger and ineffective communication result. When we honor our values, life works.

Being productive is a natural state that comes from people doing what they enjoy and honoring their most important values. Productivity and having fun are closely related.

The corollary is most often true as well. When people are not having fun, they are not honoring their values and their productivity decreases. Another way to say this is, "Do what you love and the money will follow."

By following your passions, you maximize your most productive state of mind. Doing what you love is the best way to live your core values. Developing clarity on exactly what your life rules are and which values must be honored for your life to work optimally will result in maximizing your personal power.

Carol McCall of The World Institute Group tells us that values make up the core of who we are. When we live our lives in sync with our values, we function at our highest level. When we fail to honor these essential values, we become angry and our communication shuts down.

Some examples of values are:

- adventure
- creativity
- recognition
- security
- joy
- belonging
- excitement
- peace
- intimacy
- love
- spirituality
- freedom
- happiness
- communication
- integrity
- power
- safety

And there are many more.

Ponder the list of values above. Which ones resonate as being essential to your vitality, happiness and well-being? Which ones cause you to become angry and non-communicative when they are not honored or lacking? Which do you feel you cannot live without? Distinguish between your true core values and those that may be whims, fads or passing fancies.

Your values will continually evolve as you do. When you focus on living from your values, they become honored and satisfied. This allows you to then shift your focus to other evolving values. The key to a life that is satisfying and productive is to identify your key values and make sure they are being honored. Until your life and values are in alignment, life will look like an uphill struggle.

Some examples of life rules that are tied to values are:

- If I feel I belong, I can accomplish almost anything.
- To be my best, there must be open communication.
- When I can contribute to others, I maximize my vitality.
- To function at my highest potential, I need to express my creativity.
- Without the freedom to do as I choose, life is not worth living.
- When I am happy, I am powerful.
- My dealings with others must be based on integrity if I am to accomplish anything worthwhile.
- When I am at peace, I achieve great accomplishments.
- When I access my personal power, I concentrate on contributing to others and myself.
- When I feel safe and secure, I have the confidence to accomplish any task.

When your core values and life rules are honored, you step into your power to function at your highest level. When you are not fully aware of your life rules, you may put yourself in situations where they can be easily violated.

A common source of conflict between people is one person's lack of familiarity with the other's life rules. Resolving conflicting attitudes is facilitated by educating others about what your life rules are and how they are to interact with you. When you train others how to treat you by clearly communicating what is important to you and making any appropriate requests, you will have accessed more of your personal power. Likewise, the better you understand what values and life rules are most important to others, the better you will be able to work powerfully with them.

Honoring Your Values and Living in Harmony With Your Life Rules

1) List at least four of your most important values.
2) Which are being fully honored and which are not?
3) What life rules are associated with each value and to what degree are they being honored?

4) How has not honoring these values and life rules affected your happiness and productivity?

5) What specific actions will you take to honor any that are not respected now? By when will you take them?

6) Record your answers to these questions in your journal.

15

We must continually relive that with which we are incomplete.

Mike Smith,
CEO, BridgeQuest

Completing Your Past

S ue was totally in love with Jim. The couple met in high school and dated for eight years. Everyone who knew them expected them to get married and live happily ever after together. Then Jim met Karen. Before anyone knew what was happening — including Sue — Jim had eloped with Karen, putting an end to all of Sue's dreams and expectations. Sue was devastated. All she could think about was Jim and how she had been cheated out of a happy and secure lifetime with him.

She attempted to date other guys, but no one could compare to Jim in her eyes. Sue spent her days feeling sorry for herself and dreaming that, one day, Jim would return to her.

After many years, Sue finally married another man. However, he could not measure up to Sue's memory of Jim. As a result, Sue's marriage was an unhappy one in which she never was able to give her all to her husband. After a number of unhappy years, her husband left Sue as well.

Sue lived out the remaining years of her life lonely, embittered and righteously indignant about how she had been wronged.

All too often, when something does not work out as we had hoped, we worry about or re-live the event over and over again. Maintaining our focus on the past distracts and confuses us, draining our energy.

If you, like Sue, live constantly in the past, you cannot be a whole person in the present. Your focus and energy is split because you haven't finished your business with the past, yet, obviously, you physically exist in the here and now.

It is impossible to be totally present to all life has to offer, living full out in the moment, if we are incomplete with our past. Instead of welcoming each new experience with a fresh perspective, we become bogged down in the baggage from previously unresolved issues.

Each day presents us with an opportunity to complete the past. We can do so by making a decision to resolve any unfinished business and communicate responsibly with anyone who represents any unsettled matters. By saying whatever needs to be said or doing whatever needs to be done, we can now be present to direct our focus and energies on living in the present while planning for a powerful future. When we do so, people and events no longer possess an emotional charge. Communicating responsibly with the appropriate people and releasing any remaining opinions, feelings, upsets or emotions until there is nothing left to say is the access to clearing all residue that may interfere with moving on in life. When there is nothing left to say or do and you are void of further energy around an incomplete incident, you can start anew.

Completion is a declaration you make that you are satisfied *for now* and ready to move on to what's next. When you are complete, you no longer feel the need to change, worry or fix something in your past.

There is value in declaring yourself complete at the end of each day. This declaration allows you to recognize your accomplishments for the day, putting your mind at rest so that you can start fresh the next day. When you are complete, you experience a new vitality. There is a special sense of certainty and excitement that allows you to be most productive and in the present, ready for whatever project or opportunity is next.

However, most of the time we never quite reach that level of freedom due to our reluctance to communicate all there is to say in order to put it all behind us.

Do not confuse completion with *being finished* or with *quitting*. Being finished means you have done the final step of whatever process or task you were working on. Quitting is your decision to stop what you are doing whether you are finished or not. There are times when quitting does not support you if you are quitting for the wrong reason. For example, you quit because you cannot accept an interpretation of failing or, perhaps, because you are unwilling to take responsibility for communicating appropriately what is so for you.

Although there is little room in our society for quitters, there is no dishonor in quitting if you are clear about the consequences of your decision and if staying at it no longer serves you. All there is to do is simply tell the truth in a responsible manner — and go on to whatever is next for you.

Exercise for Completion

1) Make a list of all those people with whom you are still angry or have an existing challenge or incompletion.
2) Within the next 30 days, address everyone on your list.

For those who are deceased or unreachable, write a completion letter saying everything you need to say to no longer withhold your feelings. For those you need to reach out to personally, do so in whatever manner best supports your communication with them. For some, it may be a telephone call or personal visit to say or do anything you need to in order to resolve any unfinished business or incomplete communication. For others with whom reestablishing personal contact may not be wise or desirable, say whatever you need to say in a letter. Withhold nothing. Say everything that has been on your mind, causing you to keep the communication unresolved. At the end of the letter, see if you can find it in your heart to forgive the person for any resentment, anger or sadness you may still harbor. It does not mean you need to condone his or her actions. You have simply decided to no longer dwell on these past matters so that your future can now be designed with clarity and focus. It is not necessary that you mail the letter. The power of completion will come with you releasing any pent-up emotions and consciously deciding to move on in life and leave the interaction behind, whole and complete.

3) For every interaction or situation that you experience daily, ask yourself if you are complete, satisfied and fulfilled. Is there

anything left to say or do that would allow you to resolve and put any incompletions behind you?

4) As you declare each situation complete, look to see what action, project or area of exploration is next for you.

5) Identify any areas where you have quit. Have you told the truth about your decision to quit? Is there anything left to do or say to anyone about it?

16

Character isn't inherited. One builds it daily by the way one thinks and acts, thought by thought, action by action.

Helen Gahagan Douglas,
American actress, opera singer, author, and
U.S. Representative, California, 1944-50

Living Your Life Out of a Declaration of Who You Choose to Be

Your life is the result of the ongoing process of creating anew who you are every day. Too often, people live out of the mistaken notion of discovery. This is the belief that each of us must find out who we are as a result of the many trials, experiences and lessons we experience. This notion assumes that we must passively accept and be at the mercy of whatever life has in store for us. It makes us a victim and gives us a justification for not doing, not risking, not designing and redesigning who we are and who we choose to be.

This is not to say that life is not without its lessons. We certainly experience growth and acquire knowledge from the process of daily living. However, too often we go through life tentatively, waiting for the next trial or problem to be dealt with whether we like it or not.

Contrast this with the opposite approach — living life out of a declaration describing the person you choose to be, continually reinventing yourself as you go along. When you live from the intention of designing your life on purpose, your actions will be in alignment with the image of how you envision yourself. In the moment, as you create who you decide to be, you act in accordance with this picture. The more you grow and become, the more you can yet become. There is no arriving — only the constant process of being and becoming out of your new, empowering and constantly evolving declaration.

Living your declaration is simply a matter of concept evolving into experience. Take any value you hold in high regard, such as being loving or compassionate. Until such qualities are experienced, they exist only as concepts, like a nice idea. When you decide to experience them as an acted-upon value, they take on a whole new meaning. Until you do something that demonstrates love or compassion toward another, you have only the concept of love, not the experience of it. And certainly, you haven't yet integrated it as a key principle. You have not, up till now, become the value you seek to experience.

Just as knowledge of a value can evolve into experiencing, so can experiencing evolve into being. Being is the ultimate result of *getting it* — experiencing a quality until you actually own it. This is what mastery is all about, taking a concept beyond experience into total embodiment of the value.

There was once a wise farmer who knew that life's experiences are often not what they appear. He owned a beautiful mare that was the finest in the entire village. One day, someone left the corral gate open and the mare ran off. The villagers said to the farmer, "What terrible luck." The wise farmer replied, "Good luck, bad luck, who can tell." Several days later, the mare returned with a beautiful herd of wild stallions accompanying her. The villagers marveled at what good luck the farmer had. Again, the wise old man observed, "Good luck, bad luck, who can tell."

One day, the farmer's only son was out in the yard breaking in the wild stallions. When he was thrown from his horse and broke his shoulder, the villagers remarked, "What terrible luck." Once again, as he was wont to do, the farmer said, "Good luck, bad luck, who can tell." A week later, the government declared war, calling into service all able-bodied men from the village. All went to war with the exception of the farmer's son, who was still healing from his injury. When all the young soldiers from the village were caught in an ambush and killed, the villagers again remarked to the farmer, "What good luck that your son broke his shoulder and was spared." And on goes the story.

Good and bad, right and wrong are merely interpretations that we attach to experiences. As with all opposites, we cannot have one without the other. Likewise, good health and illness are opposite states that support us to experience both sides of the spectrum. We cannot experience one without knowing the other. We cannot experience up without down, left without right, good without bad, happy without sad and so forth.

All of life's experiences present themselves as tools for our own creation. It is entirely up to us to decide how we will experience any aspect of life as it presents us with an opportunity to decide who we choose to be, given the circumstances. Instead of being a victim of what life presents us, we can choose to be the source, the creator of how we will respond and how we will be affected by the challenge. Our response is our opportunity to define who we choose to be.

Analyze the following areas to determine which ones currently support who you have decided to be and which ones detract from it.

- Your integrity level
- Your ability to make and keep commitments
- Your willingness to tell the truth in all circumstances
- Your commitment to being punctual and reliable
- Having respect and an appreciation for others
- Showing gratitude
- Taking initiative
- Living passionately
- Trusting your intuition

Living responsibly means interpreting that we are the source of everything that shows up around us in life. On some level, we have attracted whatever it is for a reason. Likewise, we have the ability to attract something different if we decide that what we have attracted does not serve us. We have the power to manifest everything in our lives. If we decide that what we are attracting to us — scarcity, illness, anger, loneliness, whatever— does not serve who we choose to be, we can decide to do otherwise. It's up to us to manifest those things that are consistent with the profile of the person we both desire and commit to become. We really do have the ability to reinvent our lives if we have the courage to do so.

Of course, once we make our decision, action must follow. Permit me to share a story. There was once a pious man living on the banks of a great river. One day, as the rains came and the floodwaters approached, the local residents were given a directive to evacuate their homes. All did so with the exception of this one man who remained, saying, "My faith in God will save me! He will provide." As the floodwaters filled the road, a rowboat approached and the boatman implored the man to get in. Again, the man declined, saying, "No need to leave. My faith will save me." The next day, as the waters rose above the first-floor level, a motorboat once again approached with rescuers pleading for the man to evacuate. Yet again, he declined, saying, "My faith will be my salvation." As the river continued to overflow its banks, the water level now totally submersed the house. A helicopter was sent, lowering a rope to rescue the man who now had climbed onto his roof. Once again, he refused the pleas to evacuate, noting his faith in God.

The next thing he knew, this pious man found himself at the gates of heaven, realizing that he had drowned. Angry and indignant, he approached an angel, saying, "How could this have happened? Why did my faith not save me?"

The angel looked at her register and said, "It's noted here that we sent two boats and a helicopter. What more do you want?"

Belief without action is self-delusion.

Living Out of Your Declaration

1) In what areas of your life — health, wealth, relationships, personal development, career and recreation — are you attracting things that do not support who you choose to be?

2) In each area, create a detailed description specifically outlining the qualities of the person you have declared that you will be, from this moment onward.

3) Living from this ideal perspective, what would an ideal day at work look like? An ideal day at play?

4) Develop a detailed vision of what your ideal life would be like. What specific actions are necessary to bring this about? Decide now to experience your ideal days on purpose living out of your declaration.

5) Record your experiences in your journal.

17

When you cease to make a contribution you begin to die.

Eleanor Roosevelt

Living and Communicating Intentionally

Gary is an intelligent, creative individual with the capacity to lead others. However, in his interactions with people, he is perceived to be arrogant and self-centered. As a result of how he interacts with others, his words never fully communicate his positive intent; people that might have been positively influenced by Gary are instead turned off. To Gary, he is being forthright and speaking honestly. He is the last to realize that how he comes across to others has cost him his power and effectiveness. When Gary speaks, people "go away" — not because of what he has to say but how he says it.

If Gary were willing to get feedback from others about how his communication can be offensive, he could reinvent his style to allow

103

his message to be heard. Doing so would dramatically increase his effectiveness.

Not paying attention to how our communication affects others is like a tennis player who hits the ball without concern for where it lands. Day in and day out, we communicate with others, unaware of the ways in which we unintentionally sabotage ourselves. We squander our power by sending messages that do not project a positive energy and image.

Through a lack of attention to our communication, we minimize our effectiveness whenever we come across in ways other than the way we intend. This might take the form of interrupting, not paying attention or not maintaining eye contact as we speak. It can involve what we say, how we say it and the energy we project. We can dramatically alter how we are perceived by becoming more aware of ourselves with respect to our communication. Our effectiveness will skyrocket through deliberate action and focused communication. Our awareness of who we are being, what we are doing and how we are communicating in each moment will result in being responsible for who we are for others.

The key to living powerfully and communicating this power is to follow your heart in answering the question "Is this communication a reflection of who I have decided to be?"

Everything about you — from your attitude, ethics and body language to your language, habits and energy — leaves a lasting impression about the person you are.

Living and Communicating Intentionally

1) Pay attention to your communication and other people's responses to determine if you are coming across to others in the way you intend. Request regular feedback about your communication. Select some coaches to give you feedback about what works and what is missing that if put into place would support you to be more effective.

2) After each conversation, rate yourself on a scale from 1 (ineffective) to 10 (powerful) as you answer the following questions:

- Did I communicate effectively as the person I choose to be?
- Did I intentionally contribute something of value?
- Do I have an appreciation of what it's like in the other person's world?
- Was I authentic and charismatic or was my energy stilted or a turnoff?

3) What areas will you develop to be more effective in your communication?

18

God grant me the serenity
To accept the things I cannot change,
Courage to change the things I can,
And the wisdom to know the difference.

Serenity Prayer,
usually attributed to American theologian Reinhold Niebuhr and
adopted by Alcoholics Anonymous

Making the Most of Your Situation

aul was an extremely gifted student. He was ranked in the top 2 percent of his class at a major university when he was forced to drop out of school to support his family. Before he realized it, his wife was expecting their third child. In order to better provide for his growing family, Paul took a job at a local factory. Although he earned only $8 an hour, he knew that he could work an extra 25 hours per week at the overtime rate in order to make ends meet. Although he could have found a way to finish school and get a much *better paying position, he found himself locked into a survival mode, unable to look beyond his daily struggles.*

Paul worked at this factory job for the next 40 years, looking forward to his three weeks of vacation yearly and the day he would retire — numb to what his failure to devise a better life plan had cost him. He failed to properly evaluate his options and find a way to both care for his family and better his lot in life. He clearly did not make the most of his resources.

The first step to accessing your personal power is to determine the facts about your current situation. When you achieve clarity on exactly what the particulars are in your life, you can then decide what your course of action will be to design your future on purpose. Your power lies in developing a plan of action starting with where you are and leading to where you want to be. You no longer will be just idly wishing for what could be.

Accepting the reality of any situation allows you to be fully aware of your options, ready to move on to what is next. In contrast, living your life from the perspective of what *should* be keeps you stuck in your opinions, judgments and evaluations of why life is not working, robbing you of your power to act decisively. Acting from choice supports life, vitality and health. Acting from obligation causes you to react to life.

When you act from obligation, you are really not taking responsibility for making a conscious choice. As a result, you are not proactive, designing your future to meet your goals and expectations. You are instead reluctantly and often resentfully acting in accordance with someone else's wishes and expectations. When you fail to take responsibility for communicating what works for you and designing your future with intention and purpose, you become a victim, subject to the demands, expectations and desires of others.

Being complete with your past and planning your course of action based upon a positive expectation for the future supports productivity and power. Analyze the facts of your situation and decide on a specific plan of action that addresses your challenges. Do not waste your energies worrying and complaining about what the challenges have been in your life so far. Take the interpretation that the past is behind you and got you to this point in your life where you can now control your destiny in an entirely new way. Your future need not bear any resemblance to the past if this does not support your excellence and happiness. You now have all the tools you'll need to plan a course that will result in a life that is intentionally designed and manifested. If you do something, do it willingly or choose not to do it, knowing that every decision you make brings consequences. Rather than complain about doing something you find unpleasant and think should be different, choose to either do it, not do it and accept the consequences or do something proactively to change it. Stop complaining and move on to what's next for you.

Exercise Your Right to Choose

1) Where are you stuck because of your opinion about how things *should* be?

2) Accept wherever you are in life, specifically identify what is next for you and act boldly and with a positive expectation and plan for your future.

3) Record your plan in your journal.

———————— **19** ————————

*F*reedom lies in being bold.

Robert Frost,
American poet

Knowing Yourself and Conquering the Resignation in Your Life

In the prior example, Paul made the choice to stay at his secure though unrewarding factory job instead of finding a better way to make the most of his options. Paul's decision to stay at the factory rather than go back to school to get his degree and a better job was based in his attitude of resignation. Paul perceived that he had lost his chance to get ahead by finishing college. Instead of looking for alternatives to improve his situation, he was resigned to the decision he'd made. Paul lost sight of his ability to still choose a better way. He became a reluctant victim of unfortunate circumstances. Paul's inability to accept responsibility for making things turn out differently resulted in a life of going through the motions, void of passion, risk and fulfillment.

In order to gain a better understanding about yourself, look at what is most apparent to you about others. Whatever we focus on in our relationships is usually true about us. Look particularly at what you find to be true and most annoying about others. These issues are typically your very own issues. Remember, we notice in other people those things about ourselves that are most in need of examination.

Your issues around the quality of your life often have little to do with actual circumstances. Your interpretations about those circumstances govern your perceptions.

We are often unaware of our ability to choose differently, opting instead to be a victim living in an invisible catatonic state of resignation. We become numb to and eventually take for granted the things we find distasteful about our lives. We adopt the attitude that this is just the way things are and we are powerless to change them.

Contrast this with the spontaneous vitality and anything-is-possible attitude that children possess. Look at how many children want to be astronauts or president of the United States when they grow up.

Little by little over the years we lose our belief that we can be, do and have anything at all we desire. Most adults live in a state of profound resignation. As we settle time and again for less than we deserve, we become lulled into a condition whereby the confining box we've built around ourselves soon begins to feel all too comfortable and familiar, too much like home. As Norman Cousins said, "The true tragedy in life is not death but that which dies inside of us while we are still living."

Resignation is characterized by playing it safe and quitting when the territory begins to appear too foreign or intimidating. It means choosing to look good rather than risk expanding when the mere possibility of failing arises. Resignation comes from the habit of living and speaking only what you know instead of playing at risk outside your comfort zone. It is only when you decide to live from a commitment to continually grow and expand, instead of focusing on yourself, that your concerns will appear petty and will be handled in light of your stronger commitment.

Whenever you are resigned, you are not being responsible for stepping into your power. Your communication is shut down. You are not holding yourself as competent and powerful. Resignation translates into blindness for exploring possibilities. Like Dorothy in *The Wizard of Oz*, we do not realize that we hold the power to return home to Kansas, the land of our dreams, any time we want to. All it takes is the realization that we are totally responsible and capable of changing any situation that does not serve us.

Conquering Resignation and Living Deliberately

1) Identify where you are resigned in life. Where have you settled for anything but the best?

2) What is the source of your resignation?

3) Where do you hold yourself as unworthy or incapable of change?

4) What bold actions can you take today to shift this false self-image?

5) Brainstorm with a coach several possibilities you had not considered to impact your resigned situation. Write your insights in your journal.

20

*When one door of happiness closes, another opens;
but often we look so long at the closed door
that we do not see the one which has been opened for us.*

Helen Keller

Complaining or Doing Something About It

Do you often find yourself complaining, griping or otherwise making someone wrong? Complaints need not be negative. If properly used, they can be powerful tools. There are times when complaints are both warranted and effective in improving some unworkable situation that may not be to your liking.

Complaints can be an opportunity to restore integrity to life. When a complaint is lodged with the person who can actually remedy the situation, it can be the stimulus to bring about necessary action. Complaints cause people to rethink and revitalize relationships by putting into place whatever is missing. They can serve to strengthen partnerships and correct misunderstandings.

However, when you find yourself complaining incessantly without taking the appropriate actions to bring about a resolution to a situation, complaining may not support you. Complaining to people who can do nothing about resolving your complaint is a waste of your time and theirs as well. Doing something to put a stop to this type of unproductive and self-defeating behavior can do much to increase your personal power.

Let's start by making a distinction between complaining and griping. When you have a prior agreement in place with someone and they fail to live up to that agreement, you may find yourself complaining about it. When there was no prior agreement and someone does something that upsets you, you are likely to gripe about it.

So, when you have a complaint, first determine whether there was a prior agreement in place. Next, acknowledge that the agreement was not kept and, finally, see if there is a request you can make or some communication you can have to address the problem and move the action forward. Perhaps, what may be needed is a clearer understanding to prevent a similar situation in the future. Remember, if you need to complain, make sure you do so to the person who can help to resolve your issue.

If instead you have a gripe about someone or something with no prior agreement, see if there is a request or communication you can initiate to resolve the situation. As Mike Smith of BridgeQuest tells us, if you find yourself frequently complaining about others or making them wrong, look to see if there is somewhere that you:

- Gossiped
- Lied
- Made a mistake and covered it up or somewhere your integrity is out of harmony
- Made some agreement you did not keep
- Are not being responsible for something

Often times, our humanity cannot accept such behavior from ourselves. As a result, we might find ourselves turning things around so that it comes out in the form of a complaint, making someone else wrong.

Any time you find yourself continually complaining about some condition that remains in place, there is usually a payoff you get for having the condition around. When you are not aware of this, it runs your life and robs you of your power.

When you do become aware of it and nevertheless keep the condition in place, you may be guilty of avoiding responsibility for your excellence. This occurs when you are more committed to the payoffs you get from keeping the condition in place than to resolving the subject of your complaint.

It is only by admitting to yourself the cost of keeping the condition around that you then can create enough incentive to clear it up. A complaint is really nothing more than a covert request. So, instead of complaining, see if there is a request you can make to add to your personal power in resolving a difficult situation.

Every complaint in your life has the potential to turn into a place where you have been avoiding responsibility for some proactive action, costing you your power, health and relationships. This situation will continue until you are willing to become responsible for dealing with the issue at hand. Complaints are the red flags reminding you that some request or action is called for to turn an unworkable situation around.

Turning Complaints Into Action

1) Each time you find yourself with a complaint, see how you can move the action forward with a request instead.

2) For each complaint, identify if it is legitimate or chronic.

3) See if you gossiped, lied, made a mistake or lack integrity in any way.

4) What must you do to resolve any chronic situation that you find yourself continually complaining about?

5) List all your current complaints in your journal. Specify a date by when you will take action to address each one.

21

*H*abits are like a cable. We weave a strand of it every day and
soon it cannot be broken.

Horace Mann,
19th-century American educator,
political leader and advocate of public schools

Training Your Thoughts

Try this test. Close your eyes and clearly picture a large
black chalkboard. Now imagine that you have very long
fingernails. As you slowly run your nails down the length of
the chalkboard, hear the scratching sound they make. Did you
sense a chill just as if you were really there doing it? If you
clearly visualized the exercise, you did.

Personal power comes with the ability to respond to any
situation with complete control over your thoughts and
actions. Every thought you have creates a physical response in
your body while putting forth energy into the world consistent
with that thought. The mind cannot chemically distinguish
between reality and a thought that is vividly imagined. That is
why people cry when watching sad movies.

Whenever you think a thought and act on it as if it were true, it becomes true for you. Repeat the same or similar thought with any frequency and it will become a self-fulfilling prophecy. All thought becomes energy that gets manifested into reality. If you want positive manifestations, think positive thoughts and do positive actions. Since you are in control of your focus if you choose to be, choose to concentrate on thoughts that support who you have decided to be. Negative thoughts, gossip, fear, envy and the like need not rule your life and command your attention, but they will if you allow it.

As you go about your day, get into the habit of asking, "Does this particular thought or action contribute to the formation of the person I have decided to be?" By developing the habit of paying attention to your thoughts, you will be bringing them into alignment with your desired being. Remember, your beliefs become programmed into your subconscious mind, generating energy that influences your reality. Replace those beliefs that do not support you with different beliefs that do and watch your world change as a result.

Take action consistently moving yourself closer toward your goal of becoming the person you choose to be. Create a vivid mental picture detailing your desired state of being. Describe what every aspect of your life will be like as though you have already achieved this state. For example, "I am a loving, charismatic leader committed to championing the greatness of everyone I meet. I listen with an appreciation for what it's like for others in their world, always in search of possibilities to make life work better for everyone as I strengthen my relationships." Read your declared vision statement at least twice a day, keeping it always handily visible. Should you stray from your path, simply recommit without judging yourself harshly for it. Take on all the qualities consistent with the person you wish to be, and you will transform yourself in accordance with your vision.

Steps to Becoming the Person You Choose to Be

1) Make a daily commitment to become more aware of your thought patterns. Pay attention to whenever you allow negative or disempowering thoughts to determine your course of action.
2) Share with others your commitment to remain proactive and focused on the positive nature of things. Ask them to remind you to focus on the positive whenever they sense you may be straying.
3) Note your observations and progress in your journal to heighten your awareness to your commitment to manage your thoughts.

22

*E*ffective people are not problem minded, they're opportunity minded.

Peter Drucker,
Author, consultant and expert on leadership design

Seizing Your Personal Power

Greg hates his job. His boss is demanding and unreasonable. He barely makes enough money to put food on the table for his family of five. He knows that he has talents that could be appreciated and rewarded by another employer but is reluctant to make a change, fearing that things might not work out in a new situation. At least his current job is secure; he knows all the ups and downs and how to get by as best he can. Someday, he tells himself, when the timing is right, he'll quit and move on to a position that better reflects his talents and potential. In the meantime, he'll find a way to make the best of a bad situation and hope that he gets a lucky break. Maybe he'll hit the lottery or his uncle John will pass away and leave him some money. Something's bound to happen.

Personal power is about the ability to trigger meaningful change and bring about a desired result in an expeditious and effective manner. There are three key elements to harness your personal power.

First is your ability to impact the world in a significant way. People who possess this power can bring about change as a result of their interactions with others. Those who have the ability to shift situations and cause others to move into action utilize this power to bring about any intended result. Instead of resigning oneself to the state of how things are, the powerful person responds to the challenge by causing the circumstances to shift to his will. He is the source of what happens to him and around him in life. Simply by realizing the personal power he has at his disposal, he is able to impact others and bring about progress in his world. This ability to influence one's environment need not be reserved for the few who naturally possess this innate talent to influence others and bring about a desired result. It can be developed by those willing to take responsibility for acquiring the necessary skills and key principles required to be maximally effective.

The second element about having personal power involves being results oriented. Either you are producing your intended result or you have a story, excuse or justification for why the results are lacking. Results are black and white. People lacking in personal power are victims of their circumstances, always at the mercy of the challenges they encounter in their daily lives. When you are focusing on the story about why results are missing, you lose your power. Your justifications for not bringing about your intended result cause you to forfeit your power to external circumstances. As Mike Smith says, "Either you are eating the bear or the bear is eating you." There is no middle ground. You either have the results you desire or you don't. End of story, or better yet, no story required.

The third important element to consider is decisiveness. People with power act decisively so as to bring about the result they intend with speed and sureness of purpose. The degree to which someone has power is directly related to the time it takes to translate his idea or intention into reality. A way to easily recognize when you are not stepping into your power is to notice the conversation you have with yourself that says, "The timing just isn't right. The best time to act is not now, but when some particular thing happens in the future. I'll wait until then to act."

This usually looks like waiting until you have gathered all the facts, or the circumstances fall exactly into place or you figure out how to carry out your plan. The problem with this logic is that *now* is never the best time to do something. If we allow ourselves to put off acting decisively in the moment, we squander our power. There will *always* be something that is not perfect or out of place to keep us from acting now. We will likely never be ready, for as soon as we resolve one challenge, another is certain to appear.

To regain your power and your ability to act forcefully, consider this. You have no access to acting in the past or the future. The only access to action is now in the present. Since it will never be the right time to act, seize your power and as Nike says, "Just do it!"

The thing that separates ineffective people from powerful people is that ineffective people wait for that one decisive moment while powerful people are decisive in the moment.

Exercise for Claiming Your Personal Power

1) In what areas of your life are you not content with your situation? Focus particularly on those areas where you have been stuck for an extended period of time.
2) List at least three examples where you have a story to justify why you have not acted already to remedy a situation that is not to your liking. What is preventing your positive movement?

3) Commit to a specific set of actions clearly addressing each of the above situations. What exactly will it take to produce a result and move the situation along in a positive direction? Set a date by when you will move decisively forward, stepping squarely into your personal power.

4) Record your commitments and insights in your journal.

23

Integrity is the value we place on ourselves. It's the ability to make and keep commitments to ourselves.

Stephen R. Covey,
Author, *The Seven Habits of Highly Effective People*

Living Authentically

John's dad scolded him constantly when he was growing up. He hides feelings of unworthiness and being not good enough. To conceal these thoughts, he projects himself as a know-it-all authority on almost every subject.

Sue was held back in second grade. She fears she is stupid and won't be accepted because of this. To compensate, she becomes the class clown in an attempt to fit in and be liked.

Accidentally, Bill nearly killed his brother in a fight when he was six years old. He hides regular thoughts that he is evil and projects a saint-like character.

127

Linda was physically abused as a child and sees herself as worthless trash. To compensate, she takes on the role of the helper, unable to do enough for others.

We all live out of images we hold about ourselves, other people and the world in general. When the image we have of who we really are is inconsistent with the image we wish others to get about us, we put on an act to conceal whatever it is we cannot stand for others to see.

Each of these people cannot embrace the images they hold of themselves. They pretend to be someone they are not and will do just about anything to avoid coming to terms with who they fear they are — which is sub-standard in some way. Of course, this is never who they actually are deep inside. Each simply has created a false concept about being inadequate in some manner. They have made up a story, which they have confused with the facts, causing them to view themselves in a less than empowering way. They've made up that they are defective, not good enough or not worthy of being loved and accepted. Because they see some aspect of themselves as undesirable or flawed, they attempt to conceal their faults and be someone very different from their imperfect self-image. Essentially, they fear being rejected and not belonging. The act they portray is often an attempt to be accepted, to merit approval, to dominate a situation or to avoid being controlled.

Each is living a lie, projecting a false façade by pretending to be someone they feel they are not, much like a bad actor portraying a movie character or a dishonest used-car salesperson trying to get someone to purchase a car they have no interest in buying. Their energy is wrapped up in pretending to be someone other than the person who they *think* they are. We sense that they are hiding something and we are left with a feeling that the person is not being authentic.

You maximize your personal power when you exude authentic energy. When you speak from the heart and your words and actions are compatible with your thoughts, others sense your genuine, attractive energy. Living authentically comes from closing the gap between who you are, what you do and what you want others to get about you. Authenticity results when who you are being equals what you are speaking. In contrast, when you project a facade that differs from what you think, others sense the disparity. When your speaking and being don't match, it keeps you from being heard and decreases your personal effectiveness.

For example, have you ever invited someone to attend an event and he said he would try to come, but something in his manner told you he would not? You perceived the person caught in a lie as inauthentic.

The answer to living authentically starts with being at peace with who you are. It's about making the decision to no longer live a lie or project an image that conceals some aspect of yourself that you are hiding.

Accessing your power means completing with your past. It's about loving yourself for who you are and not being afraid to let your guard down and allow others to love you. When your past no longer runs you, you can live with an authenticity that comes from being yourself. You then have the freedom to focus on inventing your future as you reinvent yourself on purpose.

Exercise for Authenticity

1) In what respects are you living a lie? What qualities or thoughts about yourself are you reluctant to let others discover?

2) When was the earliest age that you recall feeling inadequate or not good enough in some way? What were the facts that actually happened, free of the internal interpretations you've carried? What story did you make up about being inadequate?

Reinterpret what happened in a way that provides you with an empowering, positive interpretation of who you are.

3) Record your insights in your journal.

24

*I*n the middle of difficulty lies opportunity.

Albert Einstein,
German-born American physicist famous for his theory of relativity

Generating Conversations for Possibilities

We typically focus on finding ways to improve our daily situation and overall lot in life. This often looks like searching for methods to do things in some better, greater or different fashion, adding upon the foundation of knowledge we already have in place. As a result of this focus, we can expect small incremental levels of progress. The better-and-different approach assumes that we can add to, improve on or alter what we already have. As a result, this thinking prevents us from uncovering a breakthrough because our attention is still on what we know and presently have to work with. It's thinking *inside the box.*

Maintaining the focus on changing a problem with a better-or-different approach only reinforces the problem by keeping it firmly in place. This is typically what many consultants and therapists do. Because the attention is on altering or changing some problem, often times nothing of significance changes. Remember, that which we resist continues to persist.

Breakthroughs in our thinking or productivity will result from our willingness to explore possibilities outside the realm of what we currently know. Possibility thinking is about gaining insights in the areas of what *we don't know we don't know*. Our willingness to keep open to and explore possibilities will provide us with the opportunity to access life-changing breakthroughs.

What typically keeps us from being willing to explore possibilities is a fear of getting stuck with doing something that we are not yet prepared to take on. Separating a willingness to explore possibilities from a commitment to take action on any of them is essential. You need the space to freely explore the possibilities without a necessity to get into action. The initial commitment here is only to discovery, not action.

Successful conversations for possibilities, especially with knowledgeable, creative individuals, generate rich places to explore. Nothing is too preposterous to consider. No thought or idea is out of line. Don't be afraid that any thought is silly, stupid or too off-the-wall to throw out into the pot. There need be no limits to the imagination.

The process of brainstorming or having conversations for possibilities can be had between individuals who share a common goal, interest or background. They also can be had with people of differing experiences in order to elicit ideas outside the realm of the usual and customary thought processes elicited within a particular group or niche. Develop conversational outlets with people who don't agree with everything you say. Don't become defensive or argumentative – stay open to new possibilities, however difficult or bizarre they may seem. Remember, at this stage, you're only committing to exploration but not necessarily acting on the possibility.

Once you adequately explore with others all the possibilities that you can come up with, declare that idea-generating conversation complete and move on to the next conversation. This might be a conversation to examine any concerns around the possibility you are considering. Consider everyone's feedback, listening to what is important to each. Consider all concerns thoroughly to determine whether or not you will move into action around any particular idea proposed.

This conversation to explore the opportunity to act comes after the prior conversation for possibilities has produced an idea worth considering. Things to take into consideration include a discussion of the people and resources needed to implement your idea and who will do what tasks. If these conversations to explore opportunities and resources are not fully developed, people may be hesitant to commit to action. There is value in clearing away questions, doubts or hesitancy around what it will take to soundly ground your plan to pave the way to move powerfully into action.

Having Conversations for Possibilities

1) At work and at home, develop the habit of regularly engaging in conversations to explore possibilities around problems, ideas or goals you share with family, friends, coworkers or employees. Create the space to explore the possibilities without any commitment to act on any ideas that are developed.
2) In your journal, document all ideas that are generated as a result of remaining open to each conversation to explore possibilities.

25

T here is no such thing as a problem without a gift for you in its hands. You seek problems because you need the gifts.

Richard Bach,
Author, *Jonathan Livingston Seagull*

Embracing Problems

In our culture, we live out of a deeply rooted belief that there *are* problems and that problems *are* bad and therefore to be avoided. We are blind to the fact that labeling something a problem is merely our interpretation of what happened, not an actual event. Also, with the appearance of problems comes the interpretation that something must be wrong — with the other person, the situation at hand or even with us.

With this belief that problems should not be, are unwanted and are to be avoided at nearly all costs, our relationship to any person or situation that may prove problematic allows us little room to be powerful. As a matter of fact, we typically go out of our way to minimize our discomfort, steering clear of anything that might lead to the generation of a problem. As a result of this fearful orientation to problems, we find ourselves attaching blame, making excuses, complaining, denying, or otherwise hiding or stepping over problems in order to distance ourselves from them. Avoiding problems inhibits our relationships, our productivity and our effectiveness in dealing with others.

The invisible assumption or paradigm that we all operate from is that good people do not have problems. Therefore, if we find out people have problems, the natural thing to do is to get rid of them or avoid them as well.

This orientation to problems causes us to deny they exist or at least to ignore or minimize them. When they do show up, we tend to attach blame to someone else for them. Of course, all this hinders communication and creates suffering.

We typically are unaware of our natural orientation to problems. By being blind to it, this paradigm controls us much like a puppet on a string. We are so deeply embedded in our belief that problems are bad and to be avoided that we don't even see how this notion runs our lives.

Before we reevaluate our orientation to problems, let's look more closely at exactly what constitutes a problem. Problems only exist when there is an interruption or stop to some prior commitment. Without such a commitment, the *problem* appears considerably less in magnitude and may not even be considered a problem at all. For example, if you get a flat tire on the way to your wedding, it shows up like a significant problem since your commitment was to get to the ceremony on time. However, if you were just passing the time riding around the countryside with nothing important to do and you got a flat, it would show up more like an inconvenience.

One drawback to our orientation to problems is that to avoid having a potential problem, we avoid making commitments that present any likelihood of resulting in a problem. We play small because we can't risk the problems.

How would you act differently if you actually looked for problems because you wanted the breakthroughs that result from them? Instead of inferring that problems mean something's wrong, take on the empowering belief that problems are the source of your growing and expanding. Seek out and embrace problems as an opportunity to take you to the next level in your development. Create the expectation that you will always encounter problems and stop running from them.

Problems can actually be good! Look for the gold that lies within each one.

Consider, for example, a mathematics problem. It is easy to see how such an exercise might present a learning challenge and an opportunity to grow in knowledge. Most challenges that we label as problems offer us a similarly valuable learning experience.

Remember, the problem is never the real obstacle. Your relationship to the problem and the interpretation you create about it is. If you seek to avoid problems at all costs, you will play small within your comfort zone, not risking for fear of creating a problem. Instead, welcome problems as the medium for creativity.

Create a powerful relationship to them as an opportunity to reformulate, look for new possibilities and recommit yourself to the original commitment underlying the problem.

The Typical Scenario of Dealing with Problems
and
Why People Stay Stuck

You are in
Your
Comfort
Zone

which leads to
a return to

Justification
(I knew it wouldn't work, I really
didn't need or want it, etc.)

You Make
a Commitment

and

A Return to the Status Quo

A Problem
Shows up

which leads to

this creates

Resignation and Quitting

which leads to

Your Discomfort Zone

A Stop or
Interruption to
Your
Commitment

this lands you in

Shifting Your
Relationship to Problems

An Opportunity for Personal Growth and Development

You are in Your Comfort Zone

You Make a Commitment

Breaking Out of Your Comfort Zone

which leads to

A Problem Shows up

You Strengthen and Return Yourself to Your Original Commitment

You Use the Problem as an Opportunity for a Breakthrough

You Recommit to Expanding, Stretching and Risking

Welcoming Problems

1) Identify at least three situations that you have avoided because you have labeled them as problems.

2) What is the underlying commitment that makes each problem seem like a threat?

3) Ask yourself if you are more committed to your comfort and avoiding potential problems or to playing full out for something worthwhile?

4) Create an empowering interpretation that allows you to shift how you currently see the problems that you are now avoiding.

5) What possibilities do you see in each problem area? Which will you commit to act upon? By when will you take action?

6) Record your answers to each question in your journal.

26

T he truth will set you free.

John 8:32

I t may tick you off first.

Anonymous Addendum

The Power of Telling the Truth

For seven years, I had studied long and hard to get through college and dental school. Apparently all of the effort had paid off handsomely. I owned my own thriving practice, one of the most successful in the United States. I earned a great living, had the respect of my patients, family and peers. But something was missing. After 15 years of practice, dentistry had grown old. It had become a job, no longer a passion.

But what was I to do? Dentistry was all I knew to earn a living. And what about the sizable investment of time and dollars invested in getting my career to the place it was now? Could I throw that all away? What would others think? How would my patients get along without my care? What would my staff do? How many people would I be letting down?

I considered that, perhaps, I should just make the best of my situation and accept the fact that this was the career path I had chosen. However, to do so would be to live a lie. When I got in touch with the values most important to me, I realized that dentistry could no longer fully satisfy my need for creativity, longing for freedom and adventure and desire to contribute in a way that far exceeded what was possible for me as a dentist.

With this realization, I decided to simply tell the truth. The truth for me meant that dentistry was no longer something to which I wished to devote my life's energy. The clarity of this decision led me to identify what really was most important to me: writing, speaking and inspiring others to kill the resignation in their lives while playing full out for what was truly important to them.

Once I told the truth, things started to happen. Possibilities turned into opportunities. Before long, I sold my dental practice and embarked upon a new career following my passion as an entrepreneur, coach, writer and teacher. All this began with the courage to identify what was really so and to tell the truth.

Much of the struggle we encounter during our lives comes from not being honest with others and ourselves. We become numb to the challenges, lies and suffering that life throws our way, causing us to lose sight of a better way.

That way is simple — tell the truth at all times. Being honest with others starts with self-honesty. This involves developing the muscle of evaluating everything you say and do on a daily basis and acknowledging the lie. The lie can be anything that conflicts with your intuition, fails to honor your key values or compromises your integrity. The more you become proficient at uncovering the lie in your thoughts, words or actions, the closer you will be to maximizing your power by telling and living the truth.

Telling the truth will also afford others the permission to do the same. Remember, the truth, spoken responsibly, will not damage people. Withholding the truth will. By the same token, your commitment to tell the truth does not give you full permission to say whatever you like without regard for the consequences.

Telling the truth is not the same as speaking your opinions irresponsibly. The key is to say what is the truth for you in a responsible manner. Pay attention to your listener's apparent attitude or mindset so that you can state your truth to where it will be most accurately understood. Say what needs to be said in a way that does not damage others. Notice how your commitment to tell the truth will free you of much of the needless struggle you may now encounter.

Telling the Truth

1) In each area of life noted below, acknowledge the lie:
- Your physical, mental and spiritual health
- Your relationships
- Your work
- Your passions and recreation
- Your finances
- Your personal development

2) What actions will you take out of your commitment to tell the truth?

3) Write your insights in your journal.

27

We awaken in others the same attitude of mind we hold toward them.

Elbert Hubbard,
American author and journalist

Leaving Others Whole

S andra always prided herself in being straight with people. If she had a thought, she'd let you know about it — saying exactly what was on her mind. After all, if people couldn't handle her honesty, that was their problem, Sandra reasoned.

Sandra was not aware of how her bluntness diminished her effectiveness and damaged her relationships. Sandra didn't realize she could still be straight with people without being offensive by becoming more aware of her communication.

Once Sandra realized that her style was hindering her effectiveness, she looked for new ways to speak truthfully while leaving others whole. The result was a breakthrough in her ability to work powerfully with others on an entirely new level.

You've made a commitment to always speak the truth. So how can you honor your vow without blaming or being callous or offensive? The answer lies in speaking responsibly so that others can hear clearly what you have to say. This means expressing your thoughts with love and compassion while putting yourself in the other person's shoes. When your intent is to communicate responsibly while honoring the other person, he or she will likely be able to hear it without damaging consequences. That is, provided they listen without a propensity to be offended. Their choosing to experience what you have to say in a negative or damaging way would then not be the result of irresponsible communication on your part.

While you need be aware of speaking responsibly to leave the other person whole, it is not your responsibility to deal with any interpretations they might fabricate that cause upset. Remember, as Carol McCall says, upset is 99 percent about the person who is upset and 1 percent about the person "causing" the upset. You need not take responsibility for how someone will accept your truth. You can only accept responsibility for how it is communicated — with love, compassion, sensitivity and completeness.

Communicating Responsibly

1) How will your commitment to speak responsibly and leave the other person whole impact your conversations?

2) Distinguish between speaking responsibly and stepping over things in order to avoid a conflict or upset.

3) Take responsibility for *your* speaking and *their* listening. How can you better create a receptive listening attitude in others around you?

4) Record your observations in your daily journal.

28

As you sow, so shall you reap.

Galatians 6:7

The Power of Attraction

On a hilltop overlooking a town, an old man sat on a log by the roadside. As a traveler approached, he asked the old man, "What kind of people can I expect to find in the town below?"

The old man responded with a question of his own, "What kind of people did you find in the town from which you came?"

"Angry, dishonest and conniving losers," was his reply.

"That's what you'll find here as well," the old man said.

A few minutes later, a second passerby approached the old man. He asked the same question, "What kind of people can I expect to find in the town below?"

Again, the old man asked, "What kind of people did you find in the last town from which you came?"

"Kind, honest, decent, loving people," was his response.

"You'll find that the same kind of people live in this town as well," said the old man.

What you put out into the world comes back to you. The people, situations and events you attract to yourself will be consistent with the energy you expend. Our effectiveness with others is a function of our communication. To attract those people and things you want in your life, put forth communication consistent with what you desire. When you release positive loving energy, this is what you attract.

When you send out negative angry energy, you get this same energy in return through the people that show up in your life. Negative-minded people attract other negative people and repel positive-minded people. You cannot be negative, pessimistic and critical of others and expect to attract happy and positive people and events into your life. If you are not attracting those people and situations you desire, look at the energy you are putting forth.

We tend to notice those things in life that we think about. When you focus on empowering thoughts, you'll attract others aligned with these. Relationships reflect our energy. We see in others qualities that we like and dislike about ourselves. If you are attracting people with qualities you don't like, take a look at how these qualities show up in you. Become the ideal person you wish to attract, and your energy will be consistent with attracting similar energy. Remember that every material thing is first created as a thought before it can be manifested in the world. Take responsibility for everything that shows up around you. At some level you have attracted it. Your mind will move your reality in the direction of your prominent thoughts. So if it's joy, prosperity and meaningful relationships you desire, focus on the same.

Attracting What You Want

1) In your journal, list all of the qualities and values you admire in others and wish to attract into your life.

2) Which of these qualities are you personally lacking?

3) Develop these qualities by keeping a written reminder before you daily. Request a coach to hold you accountable to developing them.

4) In your journal, list those qualities you tend to criticize in others.

5) Turn the focus on yourself: Are these qualities that you dislike about yourself? What are you going to do to reverse the negative energy?

29

T he only limit to our realization of tomorrow will be our doubts of today.

Franklin Delano Roosevelt
32nd U.S. President

Are We Having Fun Yet?

Do you ever complain that you don't have nearly enough fun? If so, shift your orientation to what it takes to have fun. Circumstances do not determine whether or not you can have fun. How you perceive the circumstances does.

When you encounter a situation that would not ordinarily support you to have fun, look upon it as an opportunity to expand your perspective. Ask yourself, what new interpretation could you create to allow you to enjoy your experience? If you are not having fun, see if you are in choice about whatever it is you are doing. Know that you always have the option to do what you are doing or decide not to do it. Of course, there will be consequences attached to any decision.

Do you live your life as a series of constant choices? Or do you live life as if everything is an imposition? If you operate from the inner sense of "should," everything becomes an obligation. You rob yourself of joy and the freedom of conscious choice. Maybe you'd choose to do the exact same things, but they'd be motivated by your sense of free will rather than the obligation of "should." Admit that you have the power to choose. Those decisions, good or bad, are yours. Accept them.

If you do not operate from conscious choice, you will try to avoid being dominated. Your freedom will be restricted and you won't be having fun. Allow yourself to choose. Remember, no one can make you do anything you choose not to. Whatever you do, choose to do it because it is in sync with your commitment to something. When your actions follow your commitments, you'll have fun!

Exercising Your Commitment to Have Fun

1) In what areas of your life are you not having fun?
2) Where are you not allowing yourself conscious choices?
3) Where are you not being responsible for honoring yourself and your commitments?
4) What will you put into place right away to have fun? Plan at least one fun activity each day.
5) Record your insights and commitments in your journal.

30

We must not cease from exploration and the end of all our exploring will be to arrive where we began and to know the place for the first time.

T.S. Elliot,
American-born English poet, critic and playwright

There Is No Arriving

One of the ironies of the personal development process is the more we explore *what we don't know we don't know*, the more we realize how little we actually do know.

For those questioning what makes us powerful in our relationships, there is no finite answer, only additional questions to explore. Ironically, our power is anchored in our willingness to not know. For, once we know, we shut out all possibilities that fall outside of our knowing.

The process of exploring how to best access our personal power and effectiveness is a lifelong one. For this reason, the exercises presented in this book and in its sequel need never be totally completed. There always will be additional insights to be had by those willing to keep the inquiry before them.

I suggest you go back to the beginning of the book and do each exercise and reexperience each principle as though you are doing so for the very first time. Partnering with a different group of people to brainstorm and debrief each principle will produce deeper growth with new insights awaiting those willing to stay in the inquiry.

Your conscious intention to remain open to possibilities every moment, coupled with your commitment to return yourself to this intention when you notice that you are not, will provide you with endless opportunities to impact your own life and those around you. Doing so will result in reinventing who you are as you maximize your personal power and effectiveness.

Enjoy the process!

How Dare We Not

Our greatest fear is not that we are inadequate. Our deepest fear is that we are powerful beyond measure. It is our light, not darkness, that most frightens us. We ask ourselves, "Who am I to be brilliant, or fabulously talented?" Actually, how dare you not?

You are a being of brilliance. Your playing small doesn't serve the world. There's nothing enlightened about shrinking so that other people won't feel insecure around you. We are all meant to shine as children do. We were born to manifest the wonderment of the gift that is within us. It's not just in some of us, it's in everyone. And as we let our light shine, we unconsciously give other people the permission to do the same. As we are liberated from our fear, our presence liberates others.

Marianne Williamson,
American author and lecturer
on spirituality and metaphysics

Dr. Joe Rubino is widely acknowledged as one of North America's foremost success and productivity coaches. He is the CEO of Visionary International Partnerships. To date more than 500,000 people have benefited from his writing, coaching and leadership development training. Together with Dr. Tom Ventullo, he is the co-founder of The Center For Personal Reinvention, an organization that provides coaching, productivity and leadership development courses that champion people to maximize their personal power and effectiveness.

Also by Dr. Joe Rubino:
- *The Power to Succeed — More Principles for Powerful Living, Book II*
- *The Magic Lantern: A Fable About Leadership, Personal Excellence and Empowerment*
- *Secrets Of Building A Million Dollar Network Marketing Organization From A Guy Who's Been There, Done That and Shows You How To Do It Too*
- *10 Weeks to Network Marketing Success: The Secrets to Launching Your Very Own Million-Dollar Organization In a 10-Week Business-Building and Personal-Development Self-Study Course* (6 audio cassette album with workbook)

To request information about any of The Center for Personal Reinvention's programs or to order any of Dr. Rubino's books or tapes, visit http://www.CenterForPersonalReinvention.com or call 888-821-3135.

Recommended Personal Development Programs

The Center For Personal Reinvention
Dr. Joe Rubino and Dr. Tom Ventullo

Where are you stopped in your life and in your business?
Where is there an unacceptable level of resignation or conflict?
Where are there interpersonal listening and communications skills lacking?
What is missing in terms of partnership, commitment and vision?

The world we live and work in is marked by unprecedented change and fraught with new and complex challenges. For many of us, life begins to look like an uphill struggle to survive instead of a fun and exciting opportunity to grow, risk and play full out in partnership with others. The stresses, conflicts and frustrations we experience daily need not be so.

In place of these, there exists another possibility.

...To live and work in choice — empowered by the challenges of life.
...To champion others to achieve excellence in a nurturing environment that fosters partnerships.

...To acquire the success principles that support mutuality, creativity and harmony.

...To take on the art of listening and communicating in such a way that others are impacted to see new possibilities for accomplishment, partnership and excellence.

Reinventing ourselves, our relationships and our perception of the world is the result of a never-ending commitment to our own personal magnificence and to that of others. It is made possible through the acquisition of approximately 50 key principles that cause people to begin to view life and people in an entirely different way. When people really get these principles, then life, relationships, and new possibilities for breakthroughs show up from a totally fresh perspective. Through the use of cutting-edge technology as a vibrant basis for learning, growing and acting, The Center For Personal Reinvention is successful in shifting how life shows up for people by supporting them to self-discover these life-changing principles.

With this program, YOU will:

• Uncover the secrets to accessing your personal power while maximizing your productivity.

• Gain clarity on exactly what it will take to reach your goals with velocity.

• Create a structure for skyrocketing your effectiveness while developing new and empowering partnerships.

- Learn how taking total responsibility for every aspect of your life and business can result in breakthrough performance.
- Discover what the key elements are to a detailed action plan and how to reach your goals in record time.
- Acquire the keys to listening and communicating effectively and intentionally.
- Recognize and shift out of self-defeating thoughts and actions.
- Gain the insight to better understand others with new compassion and clarity.
- Learn how to develop the charisma necessary to attract others to you.
- Experience the confidence and inner peace that comes from stepping into leadership.

❖

The Center for Personal Reinvention

... Transferring the power to succeed!

Customized Courses and Programs Personally Designed For
Achieving Maximum Results

Areas of Focus Include:

Designing Your Future
Making Life and Businesses Work
Generating Infinite Possibilities
Creating Conversations for Mutuality
Commitment Management
Personal Coaching and Development
Maximizing Personal Effectiveness
Breakthrough Productivity
Leadership Development
Relationship and Team Building
Conflict Resolution
Listening for Solutions
Systems for Personal Empowerment
Personal and Productivity Transformation
Designing Structures for Accomplishment
Creating Empowered Listenings
Possibility Thinking
Accelerating Action in a Forward Direction
Structures for Team Accountability
Innovative Thinking
Completing With the Past
Creating a Life of No Regrets

The Center For Personal Reinvention champions companies and individuals to achieve their potential through customized programs addressing specific needs consistent with their vision for the future.

Contact us today to explore how we might impact your world!

The Center For Personal Reinvention
PO Box 217
Boxford, MA 01921
drjrubino@email.com
888-821-3135
Fax: 630-982-2134
http://www.CenterForPersonalReinvention.com

❖

Personal and Group Coaching Programs
By The Center for Personal Reinvention

The Value of Coaching to Support
Your Business and Your Life

In our daily lives as well as in our businesses, we typically operate from the perspective of doing the best we know how to do in dealing with life's challenges and opportunities. If we knew what it would take to be more effective in our relationships, more productive in our activities or more successful in reaching our goals, we would surely alter our behavior to correspond with these insights. The only access we ordinarily have to impact our lives comes from the areas of "what we know" and "what we don't know." In our efforts to achieve more, we usually resort to increasing what we do know by learning to do things a little better, a little different or we simply do more of a behavior that produced a certain result for us in the past. This behavior can predictably result in small, incremental increases in our ability to impact our business and our world. Likewise, by educating ourselves in the arena of "what we don't know," this knowledge then becomes part of what we now do know. As an example, if you are computer illiterate and you apply yourself to learn how to adeptly operate a computer, you will have successfully taken something that you do not know and converted it into what you now know. More than 95% of our efforts are spent in these two arenas – what we know and what we don't know.

However, our most extraordinary growth comes from outside the arena of "what we know or don't know." This includes the vast variety of ideas that we are blind to, not knowing that they even exist. It's in this arena of "what we don't know we don't know" that breakthrough or *ah-ha* experiences occur. *So how do you gain access to this fertile territory if you don't even know that it exists?*

The answer lies in recruiting the help of a coach who can support you to explore this rich domain that is outside of your customary way of viewing the world and acting upon its challenges. Your coaches should be individuals who themselves possess the key principles that make them powerful in the particular arena they offer coaching. A coach may be powerful in some arenas but not necessarily in others. The same person who is qualified to coach you in business matters may be totally unqualified to coach you in the area of relationships or spiritual matters. True coaches do not give advice or lend their opinions. They are value based, not ego based. They do not manipulate or exploit to carry out their own agenda. They are totally nonjudgmental. They are not the same as counselors or therapists. They do not try to protect, control or rescue those they are coaching. They instead listen for where one may be experiencing challenges or may be missing some key element that, if put into place, would impact a desired result. Coaches support us in gaining insights by listening both to what we say and to what we leave out. They have empathy for the person being coached but are not emotionally attached to an outcome. They serve to champion people to have their lives work optimally. They do this by asking questions, exploring possibilities, making requests and, at times, confronting issues that may need to be examined. Skilled coaching is a fine art and a highly valuable service.

For a coaching relationship to be possible, there must exist an open willingness on the part of the person being coached to undergo the process. Of course, total confidentiality must exist to allow for the freedom necessary to explore any and all areas that may need to be explored. The absence of judging and advice creates the opening needed to fully examine any possibility.

Coaching is typically undertaken in any of six major areas of life: business/career, health, wealth, relationships, spiritual or personal development or the arena of recreation and passions. A good coach will clarify if the coaching relationship is agreed to be limited to any one or more areas. True coaches are value-based and interact with honor and respect while, at the same time, they are not reluctant to call someone on their "stuff" out of a solid commitment to champion the person's excellence and best interests.

Successful coaches:

• Listen for what may be missing to accomplish a result or honor a person's values.

• Lead by example and champion others to step into leadership.

• Are committed to their client's excellence and, at the same time, not attached to his or her responses.

• Are grounded in value-based personal development principles.

• Hold those they coach as totally capable and competent while looking for what might be missing for them to fully experience their magnificence.

• Source the person coached to be their best and live with passion while playing full out to accomplish their goals.

• Never make the person coached small or dependent.

• Champion the person coached to be the best they can be with the goal of ultimate invisibility for themselves as a coach. The coach's ego must not be a factor in the relationship.

• Have permission to tell the truth and not step over uncomfortable topics or situations in order to avoid discomfort or look good.

• Create a safe atmosphere that allows for the client to be vulnerable and open to possibilities.

• Support their coaching clients in an accountability structure, ensuring that they follow through on what they say they will do.

• Support the free flow of ideas and conversations for possibilities through idea streaming.

It is helpful for any coaching relationship to begin by developing clarity with respect to the client's overall vision. This vision should include every aspect of the person's life and business. From this wide-ranging perspective, it is then possible to develop a plan to accomplish any goals. These goals would themselves comprise a component of the big picture by fulfilling or working toward one aspect of the vision's realization.

A productive coaching relationship can focus on either a life or business project. In the realm of business, a coaching relationship is often best undertaken within the context of a project or action plan that is grounded in time. By focusing on producing specific and measurable results, a coach can support a client to best work through any business stops or life challenges on route to the accomplishment of one's goals. A coach can also assist in gaining clarity on all conditions of satisfaction that may be important to a project's fulfillment. Such conditions might include those non-measurable items that would need to take place for a project to be considered a success. These might include developing stronger relationships with family members, spending quality time with children, devoting a minimum amount of time daily to meeting one's own needs, taking a well deserved vacation, etc.

Many people mistakenly assume that they can be successful in business without being successful in other areas of their lives. Our businesses are an important component of our lives, but only one such component. If there is an imbalance in any of the six prominent areas of our lives, any business accomplishment will be somehow incomplete. For this reason, a good coach will support a client to adapt a whole-thinking perspective in which mastery of all areas of life is the ultimate goal. For this reason, personal development is an essential component of any business coaching relationship. As one undertakes the personal improvement process, increased business productivity will surely result.

Just as an Olympic athlete in pursuit of a gold medal would not think of undertaking such an accomplishment without the support of a coach, most people would likewise benefit from a coaching relationship. Coaching can add fun and excitement to every aspect of life and business as one takes on the challenge of self-reinvention, always in search of excellence. And of course, one of the major benefits of an ongoing coaching relationship is development of the coaching skills that will be necessary to impact the lives of others.

If you are in business and do not yet have a coach who is committed to championing your success, I strongly encourage you to look into how such a relationship might support your goals and move your business and life forward with velocity.

Hire a Coach

The Center for Personal Reinvention offers individual and group coaching programs that support people to realize their business and life goals while designing a life of choice and without regrets. For more information on hiring a coach, please contact Dr. Joe Rubino at <u>DrJRubino@mediaone.net</u> or at 888-821-3135.

Other Books by Dr. Joe Rubino

The Power to Succeed:
More Principles for Powerful Living, Book II
by Dr. Joe Rubino

This revealing book continues where *The Power to Succeed: 30 Principles for Maximizing Your Personal Effectiveness,* left off with more powerful insights into what it takes to be most happy, successful and effective with others.

With this book YOU will:

• Discover the keys to unlock the door to success and happiness.
• Learn how your listening determines what you attract to you.
• Shift your listening to access your personal power.
• See how creating a clear intention can cause miracles to show up around you.
• Learn the secrets to making powerful requests to get what you want from others.

- Develop the power to speak and act from your commitments.
- See how communication with others can eliminate unwanted conditions from your life.
- Discover the secret to being happy and eliminating daily upsets.
- Learn how to put an end to gossip and stop giving away your power.
- Develop the ability to lead your life with direction and purpose and discover what it's costing you not to do so.
- And More!!

The Power to Succeed: 30 Principles for Maximizing Your Personal Effectiveness, and its sequel, *The Power to Succeed: More Principles for Powerful Living, Book II,* are a powerful course in becoming the person you wish to be. Read these books, take on the success principles discussed and watch your life and business transform and flourish.

❖

**The Magic Lantern: A Fable About Leadership, Personal Excellence and Empowerment
by Dr. Joe Rubino**

Set in the magical world of Center Earth, inhabited by dwarves, elves, goblins and wizards, *The Magic Lantern* is an enchanting tale of personal development that teaches us the keys to success and happiness. This captivating tale examines what it means to take on true leadership while learning to become maximally effective with everyone we meet. Rubino's fable tells the story of a group of dwarves and their young leader who go off in search of the secrets to a life that works, a life filled with harmony and endless possibilities and void of the regrets and upsets that characterize most people's existence. With a mission to restore peace and harmony to their village in turmoil, the delightful characters overcome the many challenges they encounter along their eventful journey. Through self-discovery, they develop the key principles necessary to be the best that they can be as they step into leadership and lives of contribution to others. *The Magic Lantern* teaches us such lessons as the power of forgiveness, the meaning of responsibility and commitment, what leadership is really all about, the magic of belief and positive expectation, the value of listening as an art, the secret to mastering one's emotions and actions and much, much more! *The Magic Lantern* combines the spell-binding storytelling reminiscent of Tolkien's *The Hobbit* with the personal development tools of the great masters. It is destined to become one of the classics of our time.

Have you read the best-selling book that can teach you everything you need to know about how to build a successful network marketing empire?

Secrets Of Building A Million Dollar Network Marketing Organization From A Guy Who's Been There, Done That And Shows You How To Do It Too.
by Dr. Joe Rubino

Learn the Keys to Success in Building Your Network Marketing Business — From the Man *Success* Magazine Called a "Millionaire Maker" in Their December 95 Cover Story.

With This Book You Will:

• Get the 6 keys that unlock the door to success in network marketing.
• Learn how to build your business free from doubt and fear.
• Discover how the way you listen has limited your success. And ...
• Accomplish your goals in record time by shifting your listening.
• Use the Zen of Prospecting to draw people to you like a magnet.
• Build rapport and find your prospect's hot buttons instantly.

- Pick the perfect prospecting approach for you.
- Turn any prospect's objection into the very reason they join.
- Identify your most productive prospecting sources. And ...
- Win the numbers game of network marketing.
- Develop a step-by-step business plan that ensures your future.
- Design a Single Daily Action that increases your income 10 times.
- Rate yourself as a top sponsor and business partner.
- Create a passionate vision that guarantees your success.

And More!!!

"This is perhaps the best book available today on how to build a network marketing business."

John Fogg, Founder of *Upline*® Magazine

"Joe's book is the bible on how to build a successful network marketing business. I suggest — as persuasively and powerfully as I can — that you take on mastering network marketing the way Dr. Joe Rubino has. Don't just read this book — devour it!

Richard Brooke, Author, *Mach II With Your Hair on Fire*

❖

10-Weeks To Network Marketing Success: The Secrets to Launching Your Very Own Million-Dollar Organization In a 10-Week Business-Building and Personal-Development Self-Study Course

By Dr. Joe Rubino

Learn the business-building and personal-development secrets that will put you squarely on the path to network marketing success. 10 Weeks to Network Marketing Success is a powerful course that will grow your business with velocity and change your life!

With this course, YOU will:

• Learn exactly how to set up a powerful 10-week action plan that will propel your business growth.

• Learn how to prospect your most productive niche markets.

• Discover your most effective pathways to success.

• Learn how to persuasively influence your prospects by listening to contribute value.

• Build your business rapidly by making powerful requests.

• Discover the secret to acting from your commitments.

• Create a powerful life-changing structure for personal development.

• See the growth that comes from evaluating your progress on a regular basis.

• Learn how listening in a new and powerful way will skyrocket your business.

• Uncover the secret to accepting complete responsibility for your business.

• Learn how to transform problems into breakthroughs.

• Develop the charisma that allows you to instantly connect with others on a heart-to-heart level.

• Identify the secrets to stepping into leadership and being the source of your success. And much more!

The 10-Weeks to Network Marketing Success Program contains 10 weekly exercises on 6 audio- cassettes plus a 37-page workbook.

Check your local bookstore or order directly from us.

ORDER COUPON

Yes, I want to invest in my future!
Please send me the following books by Dr. Joe Rubino.

Books	Price	Quantity	Subtotal
The Power to Succeed: More Principles for Powerful Living, Book II (hardcover)	$21.95		
The Power to Succeed: More Principles for Powerful Living, Book II (softcover)	$15.95		
The Magic Lantern: A Fable About Leadership, Personal Excellence and Empowerment (hardcover)	$21.95		
The Magic Lantern: A Fable About Leadership, Personal Excellence and Empowerment (softcover)	$15.95		
The Power to Succeed: 30 Principles for Maximizing Your Personal Effectiveness (hardcover)	$21.95		
The Power to Succeed: 30 Principles for Maximizing Your Personal Effectiveness (softcover)	$15.95		
Secrets of Building A Million Dollar Network Marketing Organization From A Guy Who's Been There, Done That And Shows You How To Do It Too. (softcover)	$17.95		
10-Weeks to Network Marketing Success	$69.95		
		Subtotal	
MA residents add 5% sales tax			
Shipping and Handling ($3.95 for the first book plus $2 each additional book $9.95 per book for non-US/Canadian orders)			
		Total	

Name _____

Address _____

City _____ State _____ Zip _____

Email_____Tel: _____

I'd like to pay by:
❏ Credit Card   Circle one: MasterCard   VISA   American Express
Credit Card Number _____Expiration Date ____/_____
Signature _____

❏ Check or Money Order Enclosed (US Funds Only)
❏ I am interested in learning more about The Center For Personal Reinvention's programs including coaching services.

Please place this order form with payment into an envelope and mail to:
Vision Works Publishing, PO Box 217, Boxford, MA 01921

Or To Order:
Call: 888-821-3135, Fax: 630-982-2134
Email: VisionWorksBooks@Email.com

QUANTITY DISCOUNTS AVAILABLE